C. J. Hurd

London, - March, 1990

START AND RUN A

PROFITABLE CONSULTING BUSINESS

START AND RUN A

PROFITABLE CONSULTING BUSINESS

DOUGLAS A GRAY

KOGAN
PAGE

Acknowledgements

The publishers acknowledge the kind permission to quote copyright material received from: Addison Wesley, Harvard Business Review and the Institute of Management Consultants.

First published in Canada and the United States of America in 1985, revised 1986, by International Self-Counsel Press Ltd, 1481 Charlotte Road, North Vancouver, British Columbia V7J 1H1, Canada.

Copyright © International Self-Counsel Press Ltd 1985

This edition, specially prepared for Kogan Page Ltd; first published in Great Britain in 1989 by Kogan Page Ltd, 120 Pentonville Road, London N1 9JN

Reprinted 1989 (twice)

Copyright new text for UK edition © Kogan Page Ltd 1989

British Library Cataloguing in Publication Data

Gray, Douglas A.
  Start and run a profitable consulting
  business
  1. Consulting services. Organisation
  I. Title
  338.7'6165846

  ISBN 1-85091-926-7
  ISBN 1-85091-927-5 Pbk

Printed and bound in Great Britain by
Biddles Ltd, Guildford and King's Lynn

Contents

Introduction

What are the opportunities?

Every year the demand for management consultants increases as our society becomes more complex. Business is becoming more and more international, and in Europe 1992 will result in expanding demand for experts who can work across international boundaries.

The flexible, decentralised firm is becoming the rule rather than the exception. Increasingly, companies are being split into strategic business units, each virtually in control of its own destiny. Unwieldy head offices are vanishing and organisations are becoming leaner as well as more compact. Companies are more exposed to the outside world, more market orientated, more cost conscious, more aware of the need to take a strategic view of the business, and more concerned with the development of human resource management strategies which are fully integrated with business needs. In the United Kingdom the market economy and the enterprise culture have combined to make businesses more entrepreneurial. This includes former public sector organisations which have been privatised. The remaining parts of the public sector are much more involved in management rather than in administration and the emphasis is on cost effectiveness.

A climate of rapid change in the business and public sector environments and in the ways in which organisations are structured and operate provides a wide range of opportunities for management consultants. This applies particularly to those who can respond swiftly and appropriately to the demand for outside expert help from the leaner organisations who no longer carry large corporate, internal consultancy or support departments.

Who is this book for?

This book is designed primarily for the person who wants to go into management consultancy or who has just started. But consultants who have been in practice for some time should also find it helpful.

Why become a consultant?

Consultants are people who are determined to succeed, who thrive on challenge and who believe in themselves.

Consultants are entrepreneurs in the knowledge field. Consultants are individuals who believe that they are competent and capable of rendering a worthwhile service to others.

Consulting offers a continual challenge and can present opportunities for freedom, growth and satisfaction far beyond those of employment or other forms of business.

What is the purpose of this book?

The purpose of this book is to provide essential information and practical step-by-step guidelines to help you to start and to develop a successful and profitable consulting practice. It contains guidance on the practice of consultancy and the basic information you need to set up and run your own business.

How the book is organised

The book is organised in two parts:

- Part 1 describes the scope for consultancy and the process of consultancy in terms of marketing and selling activities and how to conduct consultancy assignments.
- Part 2 describes how to run a management consultancy as a business, covering setting up, business planning, record and administration systems and legal, taxation and insurance considerations.

The appendices include a bibliography (see pages 228-9).

Legal and fiscal requirements

Please remember that this book aims to provide a general introduction to consultancy. Reference is made to legal and tax considerations but no attempt is made to give advice which will be applicable to your particular circumstances. Such advice should be obtained from competent professionals. It should also be noted that laws and fiscal regulations are constantly changing and, before committing yourself in any way, it is essential to ensure that you obtain up-to-date information from your advisers.

Part 1

Chapter 1

What Management Consultancy is About

What is management consultancy?

As defined by the Institute of Management Consultants:

> 'Management consultancy is the service provided to business, public and other undertakings by an independent and qualified person or persons in identifying and investigating problems concerned with policy, organisation, procedures and methods, recommending appropriate action and helping to implement those recommendations.'

What is a management consultant?

Management consultants provide the specialist advice needed when new problems or new opportunities arise that demand skills and experience not possessed to the extent required by the organisation. The advice covers anything from corporate planning to staff selection, from marketing to environmental planning.

A management consultant is someone who has expertise in a specific area or areas and offers unbiased help, opinions and advice for a fee. The help, opinions and advice are rendered exclusively in the interests of the client and can cover the provision of information, assessment, analysis, recommendations and implementation. A consultant generally works closely with the client's staff but uses employees, associates, subcontracted consultants and others as required for the project and in accordance with the agreement.

A consultant is not an employee but an independent contractor, sometimes a member of a consultancy firm or partnership, but often self-employed. He or she is contracted to perform a short-term or long-term task and is paid on an hourly, daily or project basis, or other fee arrangement.

Who goes into consulting?

Basically, consultants are people with a marketable skill, a perceptive and analytical mind, a need for independence and challenge, an ability to communicate with others and persuade them to follow advice, a desire to help others in an effective way, and a wish to be an agent of positive change. In general, those who go into consulting include:

- People who want a stimulating, dynamic, growing career that satisfies the need for personal development;
- People frustrated with their current careers, who see the solutions to problems but are unable to influence decision-makers effectively;
- People dissatisfied with the lack of challenge, opportunity or creativity in their existing jobs;
- People graduating from higher education but possessing little experience, who wish to work for a large consulting firm;
- People who are between jobs and seeking new opportunities and careers;
- People who see that they may be made redundant and wish to establish themselves in a business to earn a livelihood. These people may start on a part-time basis while still employed;
- People who have been made redundant and see consultancy as an alternative to unemployment, at least until a better opportunity occurs;
- Retired people who have expertise and wisdom to offer;
- People who wish to supplement their present income by using their managerial expertise or technical or academic skills;
- People with work experience and industry knowledge or other skills who want to combine a family life with work at home;
- People who understand government operations and the contract process, or who have built up contacts in government, politics or industry over the years.

What do consultants do?

It is possible to describe the work of consultants in terms of their area of expertise such as competitive analysis, corporate strategy, operations management or human resource management. Another approach is to view the consultancy process as a sequence of phases – contact, contracting, entry, data collection, diagnosis, feedback and implementation.

However, in his article in the *Harvard Business Review* (September-October 1982), Arthur Turner suggested that a more useful way of analysing the consultancy process is to consider its purposes, because clarity about objectives or goals certainly influences an engagement's success. According to Turner, the following are consulting's eight fundamental objectives, arranged hierarchically:

1. Providing information to a client;
2. Solving a client's problems;
3. Making a diagnosis, which may necessitate redefinition of the problem;
4. Making recommendations based on the diagnosis;
5. Assisting with the implementation of recommended solutions;
6. Building a consensus and commitment around corrective action;
7. Facilitating client learning – that is, teaching clients how to resolve similar problems in the future;
8. Permanently improving organisational effectiveness.

The basic and possibly the most legitimate objectives, according to Turner, are items 1 to 5. Management consultants are less likely to address objectives 6 to 8 explicitly, although they are beginning to approach the lower numbers in ways that involve the other goals as well. Perhaps the higher objectives should be seen as by-products of earlier purposes, not additional goals that become relevant only when the other purposes have been achieved.

Many people beside Turner are coming to believe that the higher objectives are essential to effective consulting, even if not recognised as explicit goals when the engagement starts. But they require increasing sophistication and skill in the processes of consulting and in managing the consultant-client relationship (methods of conducting consulting assignments are discussed in Chapter 9).

Another writer on consultancy, Ed Schein (*Process Consultation*, published by Addison-Wesley), has emphasised the importance of the higher objectives and the need to look at consultancy as a process in which the consultant's role is essentially diagnostic and is strongly biased towards establishing effective helping relationships with clients.

The primary role of a consultant, however, is to provide expert information or an expert service. Clients define their needs – something they wish to know, a problem they wish to solve, or some activity they wish carried out – and if they do not feel the organisation has the time or capabilities, they will ask a consultant to fill the need. This model of consultancy corresponds with the lower five objectives in Turner's hierarchy. But the higher level objectives are often the key to the complete success of a consultancy assignment, as Schein implicitly states.

Other consulting subject areas

Acoustics
Actuarial services
Advertising
Architecture
Audio-visual services
Automation
  – Office
  – Industrial
Building management
Communication
  – Electronic
  – Interpersonal
Community relations
Compensation
Conference and convention planning
  and management
Construction services
  – Heating/ventilating/air-
    conditioning
  – Inspection and estimates
  – Management
Counselling
Distribution planning
Employee benefit planning
  – Pension planning
  – Profit sharing
Energy management and conservation
Engineering
  – Aeronautical
  – Chemical
  – Civil
  – Electrical
  – Electronics
  – Environmental
  – Industrial
  – Marine
  – Mechanical
  – Mining
  – Nuclear
  – Petroleum
Ergonomics
Estate planning
Executive search
Exhibit planning and design

Food retailing
Foreign licensing
Forestry
Franchising
Freight transportation and shipping
Fund-raising
Government relations
Graphics
Health services administration
Heating
Hospital administration
Hotel and motel management
House publications
Human resource management
Industrial relations
Insurance
Interior design
  – Colour
  – Furnishings
  – Lighting
Land use planning
Landscaping
Leasing
  – Equipment
  – Transport
Library design and services
Licensing
Lighting
Lithography
Manpower planning
Mergers and acquisitions
Museum and exhibit planning and
  design
National security and defence
New product design
New product introduction
Occupational health services
Operations research
Opinion polls
Outplacement
Packaging
Political campaigning
Polution control
  – Air

- Noise
- Water

Public relations
Publishing
Recreation planning
Relocation services
Remuneration
Research and development
Safety services
- Accident investigation
- Expert witness
- Fire protection
- Product liability
- Programme design and installation

Salvage and reclamation

Security (investigation and loss prevention)
Small business development
Social services
Statistical services
Stockholder relations
Taxes
Telecommunications
Television and radio
Traffic and parking
Training
Transport
Urban renewal
Venture capital
Warehousing

Chapter 2

The Scope for Management Consultancy

Why do organisations use consultants?

Many of the factors that can affect the future of an organisation are outside its control – rapid technological developments, market pressures, demographic changes, sudden changes in the economy and the environment, shifts in political power and social attitudes.

Organisations in these circumstances need and want people who can concentrate on the opportunities and problems which they have been asked to address. Management, even if it has the expertise, may not wish to be distracted from its immediate responsibilities. Consultants can bring to the organisation their objectivity, broad experience, analytical skill and undivided attention.

Some of the specific reasons why organisations use consultants are listed below:

1. Temporary assistance
Clients frequently wish to supplement skills in their organisation by engaging trained, proved, motivated consultants on a short-term or long-term basis.

By hiring consultants, clients do not have to contend with the training, instruction and long-term commitment for salaries and fringe benefits entailed in hiring a skilled employee. Recruitment costs alone for a skilled employee can be considerable and cannot be justified for short-lived or cyclical need. Consultants are independent contractors and therefore no tax deductions or fringe benefits are involved.

2. Objective review
Consultants are retained as impartial advisers without any vested interest in the outcome of the recommendations. Internal staff may not be able to see the problems or may not be sufficiently objective. A consultant can perform a competent and thorough analysis of the issues. It is easier

psychologically for personnel to adapt to external advice rather than the internal advice of someone who may be acting out of self-interest.

3. Third-party request for problem identification and resolution

Banks are naturally concerned about any signs of a problem that might put their investment at risk. A bank may need to know whether the problems are related to administrative, personnel, financial, market or product difficulties and how the problems can be solved. Only an outside consultant's opinion would be credible.

4. Surviving a crisis

A business owner suffering from serious business problems may seek an outside consultant to investigate causes and recommend solutions.

5. Initiating change

A consultant can act as a catalyst in stimulating ideas in a highly structured organisation that otherwise might be resistant to change because of its size, bureaucracy and institutionalised nature.

6. Obtaining funding

Many non-profit organisations or small- and medium-size businesses need assistance in obtaining grants or loans for their continued survival. They may lack the expertise, ability or time to research the availability of funding and prepare a persuasive application. Consultants with an expertise in this area act as advisers or agents.

7. Selecting personnel

A client might hire a consultant for recruitment of key executives. The consultant is looked upon as being independent and unbiased with the expertise and time to screen and recommend prospective candidates selectively.

8. In-house education

Consultants are hired to provide in-house training to keep staff informed of new management and supervisory techniques or technical knowledge and to improve employee morale.

9. Dealing with internal personnel difficulties

Consultants can also be used to resolve conflicts between various levels of management. The consultant plays an arbitrating or mediating role that permits frustrations to be expressed so that energy can be directed towards constructive resolution.

10. Executive assistance

An executive who is aware of his or her personal limitations may request that a consultant review a problem, provide advice on how to deal with it and possibly follow up with implementation.

11. Government regulatory compliance

Government regulations at all levels are constantly changing, and companies are frequently not prepared or trained to comply. Consultants may be retained to provide expertise to assist a company in complying economically, efficiently and with the least amount of trauma to the organisation.

12. Socio-economic and political changes

Socio-economic and political matters are always in a state of flux. These changes present opportunities for consultants. For example, pollution problems create a need for environmental protection experts, and fuel shortages create a need for energy conservation experts.

What areas are covered?

Consultants are called in by organisations to help with any of their management problems. The main fields of management consultancy identified by the Institute of Management Consultants are listed below. Inevitably some of these fields overlap.

Corporate policy and corporate development
including
- corporate strategy and planning
- appraisal and rationalisation
- diversification, acquisitions, mergers and divestments
- image, climate and communications
- organisational and management structure
- project management

Financial management
including
- accounting and financial management
- management accounting
- budgetary control costing
- investment planning and appraisal
- treasury and finance control
- financial modelling

Administration
including
- office organisation, administration and systems
- office layout and equipment
- health and safety at work
- asset management
- office productivity
- administrative staffing and control

Marketing and selling
including
- market research
- market planning and development
- product planning and development
- sales promotion, advertising, media and material

- sales force management including sales support
-- licensing and franchising

Production
including
- production planning and control
- design and drawing office management
- quality management
- production technology and engineering
- purchasing and materials management
- plant utilisation and layout
- productivity management
- manufacturing systems

Distribution and transport
including
- materials handling
- warehouse location, layout and control
- fleet management and vehicle scheduling
- distribution systems

Information technology
including
- computer strategy and feasibility studies
- equipment and software selection and implementation
- telecommunications equipment and systems
- information/decision support systems
- information management
- systems' security management
- systems' effectiveness and efficiency

Economic planning
including
- economic forecasting, appraisal and review
- cost-benefit analysis

Environmental planning
including
- urban and regional development
- land use studies
- traffic and transport studies
- environmental impact studies
- demographic and social studies
- water and energy conservation

Human resources management
including
- human resource planning
- job evaluation and grading
- wage and salary structures including incentive and reward systems
- search, selection and recruitment
- appraisal and assessment systems and procedures
- management and staff development and training
- development and redundancy counselling
- organisation and job structuring
- organisation development
- behavioural sciences

Management sciences
including
- decision analysis
- operation research
- modelling

Technology management
including
- product design and value engineering
- energy management
- maintenance management
- research and development management
- technological forecasting
- automation including process control.

Chapter 3

Is Management Consultancy for You?

A demanding profession

Management consultancy is not an easy option. It is a tough, demanding job which requires a high level of professional skill in the process of consultancy, expertise in one or more managerial or technical disciplines, and the ability to market, to sell and to run a business. The requirements for success under the three headings of knowledge, skill and personal qualities are as follows:

Knowledge requirements
- Expertise in at least one of the fields of management activity listed in Chapter 2;
- A broad understanding of basic management techniques in the areas of information technology, methods of measurement and control, business administration, statistical analysis, and financial management and long-range planning;
- An appreciation of management and organisation theory;
- An understanding of the human factors or processes that affect the way in which organisations perform – motivation, commitment, team working, interaction, power and internal politics;
- An appreciation of the role of corporate culture and environmental factors in affecting the way in which organisations operate and can be influenced;
- Knowledge of business administration including basic accounting and legal and commercial requirements.

Skill requirements
- Analytical ability – subjecting complex situations to close and systematic examination and resolving these into their key elements;
- Diagnostic skills – examining the data produced by the process of

analysis and identifying the causes (not the symptoms) of any problems or the main factors to be considered if an opportunity is to be exploited;

- Decision-making skills – studying data and diagnoses and determining the course of action needed to overcome the problem or make the best use of the opportunity;
- Interactive skills – working effectively with other people;
- Persuasive skills – getting other people to accept your proposals or points of view;
- Communication skills – presenting your findings, conclusions and recommendations logically and lucidly by means of the written or spoken word;
- Marketing skills – assessing markets and marketing your services to potential and existing clients;
- Selling skills – persuading potential clients to accept your proposals and existing clients to agree to your recommendations.

Personal requirements
- Confidence – you must be confident in your ability to get work and to carry out assignments successfully;
- Determination – you must be able to persist, sometimes against the odds, in developing your practice and achieving the goals you have set yourself;
- Resilience – you must be able to bounce back after hard knocks (and there will be plenty of these) such as failure to land consultancy jobs, uncomfortable relationships with clients, or assignments that go sour.

Self-assessment
Many would-be consultants open a business without ever doing a thorough and honest appraisal of their strengths and weaknesses in each of the requirement areas listed above. If you have not identified your skills, attributes and talents, how can you decide which is to be your specialist area or your niche in the market? How are you able to package and sell your services, and take advantage of opportunities? Without this awareness it is difficult to project the self-confidence necessary to operate your business and respond to questions a potential client might ask you.

Many consultants never go through the stages outlined in this chapter. If *you* do so, you will gain a distinct competitive advantage. To know yourself – your strengths and weaknesses – is to have power and is a prescription for success.

The following exercise is important to help you decide the direction you should take in your new consulting business. For the maximum benefit, take all the time you need to complete each stage. Be honest and candid with yourself. The material you are preparing is for your information and benefit only.

1. Summarise your own autobiography. List and detail all facets of your past, including work positions, projects you have done, education, qualifications you have obtained, spare-time activities including hobbies and sports, family and personal relationships. Include all the work experience obtained during summers, weekends or holidays. Start with the most current time period and work backwards.

2. List all the areas of your special interest, achievement, knowledge and personal satisfaction.

3. List all your skills, that is, things that you can do. Skills are developed or acquired abilities such as instructing, administering, researching and problem-solving.

4. List all your talents. Talents are a natural endowment, often a unique 'gift' or special, often creative, attribute. Frequently a talent is a combination of skills. Think of any evelutions that may have been made about you or comments made by your friends in which your talents were observed, for example.

5. List all your attributes. Attributes are inherent characteristics such as an analytical or inquiring mind, intuition or sensitivity. Various studies have found the following attributes essential to successful consultants:

- Good physical and mental health;
- Professional etiquette and courtesy;
- Stability of behaviour;
- Self-confidence;
- Personal effectiveness and drive; that is, responsibility, vigour, initiative, resourcefulness and persistence;
- Integrity; that is, the quality that engenders trust;
- Independence; the successful consultant must be self-reliant and not conform to the opinions of others. The consultant must be able to form judgements in the areas of his or her competence and experience;
- Intellectual competence;
- Good judgement; the faculty of sound appraisal with complete objectivity;
- Strong analytical or problem-solving ability; the ability to

analyse, assemble, sort, balance and evaluate the basic factors of problem situations of different degrees of complexity;

- Creative imagination; the ability to see the situation with a fresh perspective;

- Ability to communicate and persuade, with above-average facility, in oral, written and graphic formats;

- Psychological maturity; the successful consultant is always ready to experience people, things and events as they really are with their unique individual characteristics; to view them in perspective and to take the action needed in a calm and objective manner without being diverted from a sound, logical and ethical course by outside pressure;

- Skill in interpersonal relationships, including an ability to gain the trust and respect of client personnel, enlist client participation in the solution of problems, apply the principles and techniques of change, and transfer knowledge to client personnel; a receptiveness to new information or points of view expressed by others; and an orientation towards the people aspect of problems;

- Technical knowledge, which means an all-encompassing knowledge of the business and also recognising lack of skill where it exists and seeking to acquire that skill or employing people with that skill.

6. List all the skills and attributes you lack that you believe are necessary for a consulting business.

7. List the skills and attributes you lack related to being a consultant that you believe you can improve; write down how that will happen and how long it will take. Prioritise.

8. Of the skills and attributes you believe you cannot improve, state how that will affect your consulting business choices, if at all.

9. Speak to friends, relatives or family contacts who know you well and whose judgement, candour, and goodwill you respect. Ask them to think about your strengths and weaknesses as they see them, and prepare a list. Also ask them to outline the skills, talents and attributes they believe you possess and those you lack.

10. Update and modify the personal inventories you previously prepared.

11. List your skills, talents and attributes and provide specific examples where each trait was used that could have a marketing application in providing consulting services.

12. Place in order the ten activities that gave you the most pleasure and personal satisfaction. Outline how well you did these

activities. Don't overestimate or underestimate your abilities.

13. List the top ten skills or talents, starting with the most important, that you feel are basic to your consulting practice.

14. Imagine the type of consulting projects you would like to handle and write them down in detail and why you would like to handle them. Then review your notes and identify the skills, talents and attributes required to complete these projects successfully.

15. Imagine your personal life in the future. What direction are you currently headed in with your family and career, socially, financially, spiritually and personally? What effect would a consulting business have on your existing lifestyle? Would the long hours and pressure of the first six to twelve months create strains in the family? Are you interested in marketing your abilities locally, regionally, nationally or internationally? What effect will these decisions have on you and the people in your life?

16. Think of all the consulting opportunities that might be available to you. Consultants sell themselves as people who have solutions to problems or needs, so look for problem/need situations. Focus only on existing or potential problem/need situations that relate to your area of interest and consulting expertise.

17. Increase your awareness of additional consulting opportunities by using the following resources:

(a) The Bibliography on pages 228-9.

(b) Consulting newsletters will stimulate your ideas on managing your practice, marketing your skills, determining consulting opportunities and keeping up to date on events related to the consulting industry.

(c) Magazines and newspapers; you should attempt to read everything you can relating to your speciality and general awareness of current events. Subscribe to trade and professional journals related to your area of interest. Get on all the free mailing lists that are of interest or relevant to your speciality area. Read *The Times, Financial Times, Guardian, Independent, Daily Telegraph, Sunday Times, Observer* and *The Economist*, possibly the *New York Times*. There are other newspapers, of course, that you might prefer to read, but these provide a general indication of trends and interpretation of important events, all of which could have a bearing on opportunities for your business. There are numerous excellent business magazines which can stimulate further ideas and sources of contacts and information. Browse through your local international news outlet for an indication of the

publications available. Another alternative is your public
library.

(d) Consulting and professional associations; contact with the
associations will provide you with an opportunity to obtain
information related specifically to your speciality from
newsletters, publications, meetings or other consultant
contacts. The Institute of Management Consultants' *Yearbook*
(available to members) lists consultants in each speciality in
the United Kingdom.

(e) Attending branch, regional and national meetings of your
professional institution to make contacts and update your
knowledge.

(f) Government agencies and publications; depending on the area
of your interest, you may want to get on the mailing list of
government organisations or departments that have regular
publications distributed free or at a nominal charge to the
public. The government, of course, is a major purchaser of
consulting services, and very large sums of money are
expended every year directly and indirectly for that purpose.

(g) Public and university or polytechnic libraries; there is a vast
amount of information that is current and accessible to you
for research or general ideas in your local public or university
libraries.

(h) Continuing education courses and seminars; universities and
polytechnics have continuing education courses pertaining to
business and related services. The British Institute of
Management, the Institute of Directors and other
management or professional organisations conduct small
business seminars and workshops on an ongoing basis;
numerous publications pertaining to successful small business
management are also available.

(i) Competitors; attempt to identify the competitors in your
specific field. Establish what their style and method of
operation is, how long they have been in business, how they
market themselves, what they charge and who their clientele
is, if possible. Try to ascertain why they are successful, if they
are, and how you can best distinguish yourself and find your
own niche in the market. You want to have your own
unique style if comparisons are made between you and your
competitors by a prospective client.

18. Define the consulting service areas that you would like to provide
(refer to Chapter 2 for the major fields of consulting activity).

19. Identify who you believe could be possible clients and why.
20. Project how you would like to operate your consulting business. List the important stages and time frames of your business over the next year, three years and five years.
21. List how you intend to market your services; that is, create a demand for your service and make potential clients realise that you exist. This question will be answered in another chapter, but it is helpful to go through the reflective exercise yourself.

You should now have a comprehensive, detailed and exhaustive guideline for your successful consulting business. Review it, update it and modify it on a regular basis. You should feel confident that you have developed a realistic framework for the next important stages of your business development.

Keeping up to date

Consultants must always be at the leading edge of their discipline. They should know all about what is happening now and should have a pretty good idea about what is going to happen in the future. They have to keep abreast of the latest techniques and be familiar with the newest jargon. If there is a 'flavour of the month' they should be able to talk knowledgeably about it. But they should not leap too hastily on the latest bandwagon. They must believe that there is something in it and should reject passing fads (and there are plenty of these). Above all, they must feel confident that they can use these techniques effectively to help their clients.

Consultants should also know what is happening in the world about them. They should be familiar with economic, political and demographic trends – national and international – and their impact on industry and commerce.

To keep up to date it is essential to read professional journals and the quality papers and magazines such as *The Economist*. You should also read key books in your subject area and attend courses and conferences as often as you can afford them (they are a potential source of contacts).

Institute of Management Consultants

You should certainly join the Institute of Management Consultants if you are eligible. The objectives of the Institute are:

- To provide a professional organisation for members of the management consulting profession;
- To maintain the highest professional standards of its members in terms of the Institute's Code of Professional Conduct.

- To promote the advancement of knowledge of its members in the profession of management consulting;
- To make the profession of management consulting recognised, respected and accepted through the provision of professional services of the highest standard to all sizes of organisation in private industry, commerce, government and the public sector.

Services to members

The services provided by the Institute to its members include:

- Information;
- The development and maintenance of professional standards (the Institute's Code of Practice is set out in Appendix A);
- Regional and branch activities which cater for special interest groups;
- Professional services, including the maintenance of register services which enable potential clients to contact Institute members who are members of the register;
- Training courses, seminars and conferences.

Chapter 4
Assessing Market Opportunities

Before assessing market opportunities and identifying clients with accuracy and success, various matters have to be considered.

You have to be very certain in your own mind of your area or areas of specialisation. It is impossible to target your market without this basic information. Review the exercises in Chapter 3 to determine your specific skills, talents, and attributes, and attempt to visualize the market suited to your abilities. It is important to avoid the tendency to be too restrictive in your view of the market for your services. Look for a wide spectrum to apply your services in vertical and horizontal markets and in both the public and private sector. Identify common themes and processes. Know why there is a demand for consulting services, so you can aim your marketing at those concerns when targeting prospective clients.

Thorough research is required to educate yourself and stimulate your mind on the wide range of possibilities. Read selected newspapers, magazines and trade journals regularly, and look for consulting opportunities created by political, economic and social changes affecting your area of expertise and interest.

The next chapter discusses marketing techniques in more detail. This chapter is intended to provide a brief overview of the private and public sector markets and the possibility of market opportunities.

Private sector opportunities

There are numerous opportunities in the private sector. By being aware of the issues and problems and solutions in your service area, it will be easier for you to identify and think of opportunities every time you are exposed to information through personal communication, television, radio, newspapers, magazines, trade journals or books. The habit of training yourself to be aware of marketing opportunities at all times is essential.

It is important to understand the motivating factors that will cause a potential client to want your services. You might be very aware of the needs of your service within your speciality area, but a client who does not recognise that your service is needed will not be receptive to your offer of assistance.

There are many reasons that motivate a client to retain a consultant, but three of the basic reasons are: to obtain information, to save time and to save money. If you can visualise the ways you can save a client time and money, and provide the most current and accurate information in the client's area of interest and need, market opportunities in the private sector will be considerable.

Individuals

Individuals buy the services of consultants in a wide variety of fields. A study of the Yellow Pages or business telephone directories should provide a good example. Advice on how to save money or how to make money is fairly common. In this instance, the target market is anyone in the higher earning bracket, including executives and professionals. Some examples of consultants in this area are tax consultants, financial consultants, investment consultants and property consultants. Other consulting areas include interior design and fashion.

Small businesses

Small businesses provide an excellent client base for a new consultant. The failure rate of small businesses is very high. Lack of knowledge by the small business owner/operator in important areas of small business management is often a factor. If your skills include small business management and how to make money or save money for a small business owner, you can find a market. There are numerous books available on business management that will provide ideas for you. Some are included in the Bibliography on page 228.

Various techniques can be used to attract small business clients. You can offer a fee based on percentage of savings or profits that occur as a result of your advice. Naturally, you would have to have a measurable basis for showing the positive benefits that your advice has created. A percentage fee is a good marketing device. It shows confidence in yourself, and it is a difficult offer to refuse as your payment is based on performance.

Another need of small businesses is to raise funds, either through the venture capital market, commercial banks or government grants and loans. Most small businesses go through growing pains. Wherever business growth occurs, problems occur, and wherever problems occur, a need exists for solutions.

Medium-size businesses

There is a big demand for consultants in medium-size businesses. Companies often use experts as required instead of taking on staff. Staff involve the related costs of training, benefit packages and long-term commitments for possibly short-term needs. Businesses are vulnerable to economic changes, and their survival is based on keeping overheads low and making a profit. Any areas of need you can identify to increase efficiency and productivity and sales, and decrease overheads and losses, will create a demand for your services.

Medium-size businesses are also constantly going through various stages of growth with all the predictable problems involved.

The advantage of dealing with a medium-size business is that projects tend to be more lucrative. There is also a greater chance of repeat business. Another advantage is that the decision-makers are generally more sophisticated, better able to see the need more readily, more accustomed to dealing with consultants and able to respond more quickly on proposals.

Large companies

It is more difficult for sole practitioners or small firms to obtain contracts from larger companies. Many large companies prefer dealing with large consulting firms or well-known consultants with considerable experience and contacts.

Because of the money available in larger businesses, consulting opportunities do exist, particularly in the area of temporary technical assistance. It is common for consultants to large companies to have developed their experience and confidence with smaller and medium-size companies before approaching the larger companies.

Public sector

Government is a major user of consulting services. Marketing opportunities are available in various forms in the public sector; ie, national and local government agencies and the public agencies, and nationalised industries that have not yet been privatised. You can submit a solicited or unsolicited proposal and attempt to get the contract directly.

If you are considering the public sector as a source of business, you should be aware of the various ways of obtaining contacts or information to assist you. You should also have an understanding of the way government departments and other sectors operate. The Department of Trade and Industry is an important source of business. In March 1989 some 2500 consultants were involved in DTI schemes.

Making contacts and obtaining information

There are various steps you can take to obtain the necessary information and make the necessary contacts to assist you in your government dealings.

(a) Read government advertisements and publications pertaining to your areas of interest.

(b) Place your name on mailing lists. There are numerous government departments and you can request that your name be placed on each list to receive all relevant information, including proposed procurements and contracts awarded relating to your field.

(c) Attempt to have your name placed on sourcing lists as a consultant in various speciality areas.

(d) Contact government contract officers. Most government contracts are awarded at the department or agency level where the specific needs are best known and money has been allocated. The phone book has listings for various branches of government. The public library has updated lists of all the key government departments, individuals, their titles and phone numbers. Once you have obtained the correct department, ask to speak to the contract officer who can provide you with further background.

(e) Visit government departments and agencies. After you have submitted your curriculum vitae to various government departments, you may wish to meet the person in charge of contracts approval and introduce yourself. This may or may not be appropriate or possible, depending on your geographic location and government policy. Keeping contact with the key person who could award a contract shows your interest in keeping your name current. It also demonstrates initiative and confidence. On the other hand, over-persistence can cause irritation.

(f) Contact large consulting firms that are the recipients of government contracts and require additional consulting assistance for those contracts.

(g) Contact other companies that have recently received a government contract. You can then determine what subcontracting opportunities might be available in your area of speciality, and immediately contact the companies concerned.

(h) If you have friends or acquaintances who work in government, tell them you are looking for consulting assignments in your speciality. You should also provide them with your curriculum vitae and brochure if possible. They might be in a position to inform you if they hear of an agency in need of your services. You might therefore hear of a need before the department has advertised for services or selected a consultant. You can then submit an unsolicited proposal.

International agencies

If you are interested in overseas work – and the developing countries provide massive opportunities for consultants – make contact with the various agencies.

The most important source of funds for overseas work is the World Bank. Their contracts are most frequently awarded to the big consultancies and consortiums, but if you feel you have something special to offer, it would be worth contacting them direct.

Other international organisations who use consultants include the United Nations, the International Labour Office, the World Health Organisation and UNESCO.

Large consultancies

The large consultancies may find themselves short of particular skills – good consultants are hard to come by. They therefore occasionally subcontract work and it is well worth your while to establish contacts with one or more firms to make them aware that your expertise is available.

Chapter 5

Marketing Your Consulting Services

Introduction

Marketing is an essential process for success in the consulting business. Marketing is a process that involves a wide spectrum of activities, ultimately directed at convincing prospective clients that their needs can be met and their problems can be solved through your specific services. Selling is a part of the marketing programme. It is intended to result in a consulting assignment by means of personal interaction begun at the initial meeting and maintained during and after the assignment.

The dynamics of the marketing/selling stages have to be clearly understood and carefully cultivated by the consultant. For example, when you are marketing yourself, you have carefully to calculate the image that you want to project when you are packaging your product, ie yourself, and your services. You and your marketing efforts must project authority, confidence, friendliness, candour, expertise, competence and leadership.

Many consultants fail, or maintain a marginal income, because of poor marketing. Consultants frequently do not appreciate the necessity of marketing, do not know how to market, do not like to market, do not want to market or do not take the time to market.

Business objective

Your objective will be to maximise profit by achieving high utilisation rates (percentage of chargeable time – aim for 75 per cent with a minimum target in the first year of 50 per cent) charging the maximum fees the market will bear, and minimising expenses and tax liabilities.

Marketing plan

In your marketing plan you should:

1. *Define your skills and services.* This is covered in Chapter 3. You should have a clear idea now of the nature of the services you will

be offering potential clients. You may have decided on just one particular area of interest and speciality, or you may have decided on several areas that you will promote as unique areas, either to the same client or to different categories of clients.

2. *Target prospective clients.* Identifying possible client consulting opportunities is the next step in the marketing plan. This was covered in Chapter 4.

3. *Make the public and potential clients aware* of your services and create a demand. The various techniques required for this step are covered in the next section.

4. *Follow up leads.* Naturally, once interest has been aroused by your effective marketing, you must quickly follow up the lead to arrange a meeting.

5. *Meet prospective clients.* There are basically two sorts of meeting:

   (a) when you follow up a general lead and your tasks are to identify the client's needs and to decide how you might help;

   (b) when you are responding to an invitation to 'pitch' for an assignment, probably in competition with other consultants. In this case you may obtain all the information you need to prepare a proposal at a single meeting. Alternatively, it may be necessary to conduct a more extended survey, which might or might not be paid for by the client.

   Methods of conducting client meetings and carrying out surveys are considered in Chapter 6.

6. *Prepare the proposal.* If the first meeting with the prospective client has been purely exploratory, your proposal may simply outline your understanding of his or her situation, the help you could provide and the benefits to him or her of giving that help. If, however, you are pitching for a specific assignment, you would set out in detail your definition of the problem, how you intend to solve it, how and when you will do the work and how much it will cost. Methods of preparing proposals are given in Chapter 7.

Marketing techniques

The main marketing techniques you should consider using are as follows:

- networking
- brochures
- direct mail
- advertising

- membership of professional, trade or business associations
- donating your services
- attending public and professional meetings
- lectures
- teaching
- seminars and workshops
- free media exposure
- radio and television talk shows
- letters to editor
- writing articles
- writing a book
- having articles written for you
- announcement columns
- newsletters
- use of a PR consultant
- registration.

Networking

You need to develop and maintain a contact network to establish leads, attract invitations to carry out consultancy projects or to pitch for assignments, and to add names to your mailing list. It is perhaps the most effective way to acquire clients. Studies have shown that the majority of a consultant's clientele come from referrals through a contact network or from satisfied clients.

A contact network is a collection of associates, friends, acquaintances and other people you meet in the course of business or socially. You already have many and you can cultivate many more. The list will include past and present clients (an important source of business, which is treated separately below), former employers or professional colleagues, business associates, other management consultants, bankers, lawyers, accountants, friends, neighbours and relatives. These will include any contacts you develop through commercial or business associations – hence the importance of joining your own professional association(s) and taking an active part. Apart from the mainstream associations such as the Institute of Chartered Accountants, the Institute of Marketing, the Institute of Personnel Management and the Institute of Management Consultants, there are bodies such as the Institute of Directors and the Royal Institute of Public Administration that may be worth joining. If you sit down and list everyone you know who comes to mind as a potential contact, the list will be longer than you think.

Networks have to be maintained as well as developed. If you get to know someone, keep in touch. Make him or her aware of the fact that

37

you are available if required. Don't be too pushy, but telephone or write a letter if you have done or are doing something which might be of interest. Send him or her updated copies of your brochures, press cuttings referring to work you have done or a lecture you have given, or copies of any journal articles you have written. Even if you do no more than send something with a compliments slip attached simply saying 'This may interest you', it will be a means of reminding him or her of your existence.

Networking is the most effective and inexpensive way of increasing your exposure and credibility. Continually update your network by adding leads and other contacts to your mailing list.

Clients

Networking is important, especially when starting, but consultancy is essentially about building up the client list. Repeat business can be a major source of fee income, although you should try to avoid becoming over-dependent on one or two clients. If for any reason that source of work dries up you could be in serious difficulties. You must continually seek to add potential clients to your list.

Cultivating former clients involves treating them as a special category of your network. Assuming that they were satisfied with your services, they will be inclined to go back to you if a new problem emerges in your field. After all, they know you, and you know them. There is no learning curve. You can plunge straight in. But don't wait for them to come to you. Keep in touch – subtly.

Obviously, you will be seeking additional work from your existing clients. Help with implementation is the ideal approach. If you are around, even if only periodically, an opportunity may emerge for a new assignment. At least, if you are glad to help with implementation this will overcome the criticism frequently made about consultants, and not always unfounded, that they come along to make their *ex cathedra* pronouncements and leave the client to put into practice their theoretical recommendations, while they move on swiftly to 'fresh woods and pastures new'. But in seeking repeat business don't give your client the opportunity to repeat the old gripe about consultants – that once you get them in, you can't get rid of them. The additional work must be something which the client really needs doing and from which measurable benefits will flow. And you must have the capability and capacity to do that work.

Other management consultants

Your network should include other management consultants – the big firms (if you can make contact) as well as the smaller ones. If you are a sole practitioner you should make a particular effort to link up with other sole practitioners. They could be in your own field, or closely associated ones, or they could be in a different but complementary area.

Associations of this kind can generate work of 'the taking in each other's washing' variety. If actual work or a lead comes to you which you cannot respond to – either because it is not in your field or you are already fully committed and the client cannot wait – then you can pass it on, and vice versa. There may be occasions when a joint approach is desirable, either to provide the necessary range of skills or to cope with the workload.

Such arrangements can be entirely informal.

Brochures

Brochures are a very important part of marketing your practice. There are many ways to use a brochure.

1. Leave it with a prospective client after a meeting.
2. Mail it after a written or formal request for further information.
3. Send it in a direct mail campaign targeted to prospective clients.
4. Distribute it at a seminar or presentation you are giving.
5. Send it out the next day to those who attended a seminar or presentation as a form of follow-up communication.

Keep in mind that your brochure is probably the first contact a prospective client has with you and the services you offer. The reaction to the brochure may be positive or negative, depending upon its format, content and quality. Here are some tips on preparing a brochure.

(a) As the first impression of the brochure is critical, it is important that the layout, graphics and paper are of first quality. You want to stimulate a desire in the recipient to retain you as a consultant, or at least to enquire further.

(b) The size and format of your brochure is a matter of choice. But it should not be too long. You don't want to bore your readers. If you can have an attractive cover and say all you need to say in four 8 x 5in pages, so much the better.

Obtain advice from typesetters and graphic artists and printers before you finish your draft. Seek out comparative opinions and quotes until you are satisfied with the quality and cost offered.

(c) The phrasing of the text should reflect a confident, positive, dynamic yet professional tone. Have the spelling, grammar, syntax and style of your text checked by someone with relevant skills.

(d) The text should be concise, clear and brief. Text in point form can be easily read. Refrain from using long or complicated words. Keep the words simple and direct. Focus on the benefits that a prospective client will receive from your services. Draft the text from the viewpoint of the client's needs.

(e) Provide information on the history of your business, the nature of your business, your clientele and the type of services you perform. Explain why a particular service might be required. Explain or list the benefits that you can give to provide the service and meet the need or resolve the problem. Think of previous clients who benefited from your advice and assistance.

(f) List your academic and professional achievements and experience.

(g) Do not list your associates unless you have a long-standing relationship or know that they will be staying with you for an extended time. Refer to the resource base of talent your firm offers. You may wish to itemise the skills that are provided by key associates.

(h) A list of important clients should be included in the brochure.

(i) Many consultants prefer not to have their photograph in the brochure, as a matter of personal choice and style. The reaction of a potential client to your photograph could be negative or positive based on your picture alone.

The design of the brochure should be consistent with your stationery and business cards.

(j) Before you have the brochure printed, ask a number of your friends, relatives and business associates to look at the draft copy of the brochure and obtain their candid opinions.

Direct mail

Direct mail can be a very effective means of making potential clients aware of and interested in your services. There are several advantages to direct mail: the cost is flexible, the sales message can be personalised to the needs of that particular target group, and the letters can be individually addressed to specific persons on a word processor. An important cost/benefit aspect is the controlled circulation to a selected audience.

The first step is to develop and/or acquire a mailing list. The most cost-effective way may be to build up your own list consisting of contacts and past and present clients. But it may pay you to extend your target audience by renting a list.

Mailing lists are often rented from list brokers for one-off use, and are 'seeded' by means of fictitious companies or individuals to ensure you do not use the list longer than the time contracted. For further information consult the *Direct Mail Directory* of *British Rate and Data (BRAD)*.

The various directories of organisations related to your speciality may also rent or sell mailing lists. The advantage of this type of mailing list is that prospective clients may be members of the organisation that publishes the directory. You would therefore be targeting your services to your specific trade or interest market.

There are a number of specialised direct mail advertising agencies listed in *BRAD*. For a fee, they will determine the best mix of mailing lists for your purpose, depending upon the amount of money you are prepared to budget. They can obtain the best rates for you and for an additional fee will prepare your mail shot, but this can be expensive.

Response rates can be very small – less than 1 per cent unless you have a very specific and well-presented proposition which is sent to a highly selective list. Many other factors will decide your response rate, such as the type of consulting service you provide, the economic climate at the time, the cyclical or seasonal demand for your type of service, and the techniques and format you use in the direct mail approach.

There are various stages involved in direct mailing, all of which are equally important to obtain the desired objective. The basic steps are as follows:

(a) Your first mailing should be within the regional area you can realistically service. It is also an opportunity to test-market and analyse the effectiveness of your mailings without spending a large sum of money.

(b) Your mailing should consist of a personalised covering letter (on a word processor if available) and sent directly to the key person who is the decision-maker. Use quality letterhead stationery to create a professional impression. Enclose a copy of your brochure with your letter. Outline briefly the services you offer and the benefits that will be obtained by the prospective client. State that you will contact the client within five calendar (or business) days to answer any questions and discuss the matter further at that time.

(c) Keep an accurate filing system of all prospective clients you intend to follow up. List all pertinent information on the card

41

so that you can review it and familiarise yourself with it before you contact the client. Note the date in your daily diary or calendar to remind you to contact the prospective client on that date.

(d) Follow up with a telephone call five working days after you post the letter. This will create a positive impression with the client with regard to your administration and professionalism. Follow the phone call with a visit to the prospective client if circumstances allow. The next chapter outlines other procedures and techniques to follow before, during and after the first meeting with the prospective client.

(e) If the response to your mailing is poor, review all your techniques and format thoroughly. This includes the direct mail target group, covering letter, brochure, telephone techniques and meetings.

(f) Constantly revise, refine and upgrade your mailing list with new prospects.

(g) Send out mailings on a quarterly basis (or more often), as your finances, marketing plan and other circumstances dictate. This will remind people of your services and expertise, and the repetition ultimately does have an effect. When sending out repetitive mailings, consider enclosing a newsletter, which you could easily prepare, and copies of any articles or other papers pertaining to the industry that is your target base. You may want to have a tear-off feature in the newsletter offering a free subscription to the newsletter if a request is sent to be kept on the mailing list. This way you should be able to track the response. Over time, a large portion of qualified prospects should respond to regular and consistent promotional efforts.

Advertising

Most consultants are reluctant to use advertising to develop the practice either because it is not cost-effective (and it seldom is) and/or because they feel that it is unprofessional. Most clients select a consultant by reputation, but it depends on the nature of your consulting business. For example, if you specialise in small business cash flow problems, and in your region there are small businesses with problems, you might put a tasteful, professional advertisement in the display ads in the business section or the classified section of your local newspaper to stimulate interest.

The cost/benefit equation may be more favourable if you advertise in a trade or professional journal where at least you can target your audience. This may often be the case if you are advertising a seminar or training programme, but you should be very certain that you are going to get results before you place a general advertisement about your services.

Membership of professional, trade or business associations

Joining a group and then actively participating in meetings and other functions is an effective means of developing leads. Try to attend meetings on a regular basis and get involved in discussions. Evaluate a group or association on the basis of potential consulting prospects who are active in the association. You want to look for members who are likely to give you consulting opportunities. Because of the time commitment involved to develop your reputation within an organisation, you must be very selective in your membership. Limit your memberships to one or two. You may wish to consider such civic or trade organisations or associations as the Chamber of Commerce, Rotarians, Lions, or associations directly related to your service area. Obtain a list of all the members of the organisation and review the list thoroughly. Most lists provide the name, position and company, type of business or profession of the member, and address.

Donating your services

You may wish to donate some consulting time and commitment to a worthwhile non-profit organisation as a gesture of goodwill. Naturally, you have to be very cautious about the time involved relative to the potential benefit, but your services without charge can enhance your image and result directly or indirectly in referrals.

Attending public and professional meetings

Consider attending meetings covering a subject directly or indirectly related to your field of expertise. You want to see and be seen. Plan to contribute your opinion, if appropriate, in a well-planned, concise and intelligent fashion. Prospective clients could be attending the meeting. Try to identify and talk to people you believe are worthwhile contacts.

Lectures

Many organisations or professional associations need speakers for their conferences, seminars and training programmes. Find out who organises them and get in touch in order to suggest subjects which you could talk about. Fees, if any, may not be high but the publicity is invaluable.

You can spread your net even wider by contacting organisations or associations who need speakers for meetings or at luncheons or dinners. When you contact the programme chairman, offer your services free, and advise him or her that you have a number of prepared talks you believe would be of particular interest to the membership. Mention that your subject areas are topical and interesting, and your talk can be between 10 and 30 minutes long. This is the normal range of time required for a speaker. Ask about the mix of membership and the number of members who normally attend meetings. Try to acquire a list of members to review in advance so that you can direct your comments more accurately towards your group.

It is helpful to have ready two or three 10- to 40-minute presentations with supporting material. You will then be available at short notice for any presentation.

The object of the presentation is not necessarily to make money, but to obtain contacts and increase your credibility and exposure for future consulting opportunities. Those who attend will probably tell their friends or acquaintances about you if your presentation is interesting. Make sure you tell the audience that you are a consultant. During your presentation you can give a number of examples or tell anecdotes based on your experiences. This will reinforce your image as an expert. People will remember you better by the examples or stories that you relate.

Books related to public speaking and effective presentations are listed in the Bibliography on page 228.

Teaching

There are many opportunities to offer your services as a part-time or occasional lecturer on professional courses in your field run by polytechnics and other colleges of further education. You are generally paid for your time, but ideally the students who attend the course will be potential clients or will recommend you to friends or associates. Make sure that you teach adults only to maximise the potential benefit. You are primarily looking for credibility, exposure and contacts. The preparation required to teach a course also keeps you up to date on your subject area.

Seminars and workshops

Depending upon your area of expertise and the size of your target market, you may wish to consider offering your own seminar or workshop at a nominal charge. The people who attend are excellent potential clients. You should try to select a subject that allows you to provide a practical overview of important tips and ideas within your speciality area. You can promote your seminar through your direct mail list. Allow four to eight weeks' lead time to ensure that people are not already booked up.

Other items to consider are the length of the seminar, the location, the time, whether day or evening, when refreshments would be served, if any, and the number of people you can accommodate. Make sure your announcement states that it is limited, advance registration only.

In your announcement you can request that registration be made by telephone one week in advance of the seminar. This will give you some idea as to the response, and assist you in the preparation of your material.

You may also wish to consider advertising possibilities in the local newspaper and other monthly or weekly publications.

If you have a deadline for registration one week before the seminar, and not enough people appear to be interested, you can try to negotiate a cancellation arrangement with the hotel facility by paying a portion of the room rent, or possibly nothing at all if the hotel is able to rebook the facility.

Make sure you distribute your brochures, newsletters and any other appropriate material at the seminar. Develop a seminar evaluation form with questions that will provide a good source of biographical information on the participants, opinions of you and your seminar topic through means of rating scales, and space for additional comments. Provide a coupon on the seminar evaluation form for participants to complete if they wish to be kept on your mailing list for newsletters. Also have a space on the form for asking what particular areas of interest or concern a participant might have. This should assist you in developing other seminars or improving the existing one.

When a person phones in to register prior to the seminar, as well as on the day of the seminar, make sure that you get the full company name, address, phone number, and name and position of the person attending. You will want this information for your mailing list. For further information on conducting seminars and workshops, refer to the books outlined in the Bibliography on page 228.

Free media exposure

There are many devices for obtaining free media exposure. Exposure provides credibility for you, and develops an awareness in the public that you are an expert or authority in one or more areas. If a seminar or presentation is offered, either through your own company or through some other organisation, consider preparing a news release. Send it in advance to the appropriate radio, television, newspaper or magazine contact person. Find out who the contact person is and phone in advance so he or she will be expecting your letter or news release. It also gives you an opportunity to introduce yourself and to make sure that the approach you are adopting will obtain the desired free exposure.

Ask the contact person what format is preferred for the information required. Spell out in your letter, and in your conversation, why you feel the topic of the presentation is of interest to the readers, viewers or listeners. The subject matter may be topical or controversial.

Radio and television talk shows

The previous point dealt primarily with announcements of forthcoming presentations. An extension of that exposure is to appear in person on a radio or television talk show. The same approach applies as in free media announcements. Locate the appropriate contact person and explain the benefits to the listeners or viewers of your being interviewed on the programme. If possible, try to be on the programme a week before your seminar or presentation, in order to stimulate attendance. If the talk programme is too distant from the seminar date, the listener may forget about it.

Letters to the editor

It is not too hard to get published in the 'letters to the editor' section of a magazine or newspaper. Write a letter that is topical and relevant and reflects a controversial or divergent opinion. Refer to an earlier article if you are reacting to something previously published. Mention in the letter that you are a professional consultant in the field and have expertise in the subject area.

Writing articles

Writing is an effective way of developing exposure, credibility and contacts. Once you have developed the format, style and discipline, you should be able to write three or more articles a year for various publications. All publications are looking for articles; many do not pay very much, if anything, for unsolicited articles – but they are frequently published.

To locate magazines that have your target audience, look in your local reference library at *Willings Press Guide, British Rate and Data* and the *Writers' and Artists' Yearbook*.

Write an article about your area of expertise that you believe would be of particular interest to the readership of the publication. Use examples and stories in your article. The subject matter could deal with new trends, the effect of pending legislation, technical information, or any other angle that will enhance your image as an expert.

Contact the publishers of the magazines or journals and obtain free copies so you can study them and familiarise yourself with their style and length. If your article is accepted for publication, request a by-line and a brief biographical comment at the end of the article. Say that you are a consultant in your area of expertise, and invite questions or comments about the article. Not all publications will permit this.

There are numerous books on writing style. Some of them are listed in the Bibliography on page 228. Have your article reviewed by at least one, if not two, friends or relatives who will comment candidly. Submit a good quality 5 x 7in glossy photograph of yourself and a biography with the article. Submit the articles one at a time to the editors of several trade journals and business magazines whose readership constitutes your potential target base. If your article is published, obtain extra copies from the publisher to distribute in your next direct mailing or presentation.

There is an additional benefit to writing articles. The research process is an excellent way to develop contacts and credibility. For example, you could carefully select 20 or 30 people to interview for background information for the article. These people could include key potential clients. You can telephone them, in which case have a script ready before you phone them. Ask open-ended questions, listen carefully and note their answers. Prepare follow-up questions for their responses. This should show that you are knowledgeable and an intelligent communicator. When you contact the prospective client over the telephone, introduce yourself as a consultant writing an article. You can ask their opinion on such matters as the effect of pending legislation, unique problems they encounter in their field of interest, and major opportunities or trends they perceive. Preferably, you can arrange to interview them in person. At such interviews it is best to record the discussion on tape.

Research implies analysis, and your analysis should be thorough. The telephone conversation can be followed by a letter on your stationery thanking people for their cooperation and assistance. Depending upon the responses to your questions, you may see that many consulting opportunities exist with the people contacted. They may have mentioned some of their problems. At a comfortable time in the future, you may wish to contact these sources and follow up with a personal letter and brochure. Subtlety is essential – you must not lay yourself open to the charge that your original contact was made under false pretences. Your research must have been genuine.

Writing a book

Having a book published is another marketing technique to establish yourself as an expert in your field. There are, however, a number of limitations. You have to find a publisher for your book or publish it yourself, which can be expensive. Your book could be obsolete by the time it is published, as the lead time before publication can be considerable. The time you would have to spend on the book might not be justified in terms of the cost/benefit, because of loss of income or potential income. It could be far more beneficial to spend the time writing articles rather than a book. Regular articles also keep your name in front of the public and reinforce your image as a specialist.

Have articles written about you

Every field of consulting has news value. By carefully cultivating relationships with editors and reporters, you could be looked upon as being an expert in your area. They might invite your opinion and quote you in an article on the topic. You could also have articles written about you, if you can demonstrate the newsworthy feature, topical benefit or uniqueness. Try to look for news angles that could have a direct or indirect effect on the public at large or your target group in particular. Look at economic, social, political or legislative factors. Over time you could build up a reputation as an authority that will generate enquiries from prospective clients.

Announcement columns

Many professional, trade or university graduate publications have sections devoted to announcements of interest about their members. Make a point of regularly updating information provided to these publications whenever you can find an excuse to justify it, if your style allows. Such things as having given a presentation, expanding the services that you provide, or announcing new associates or distinctions can get your name inserted. If you are giving a seminar or workshop, give yourself enough lead time for an announcement to be inserted, if possible, in these publications. Various publications of a daily or weekly nature may have a free announcement section available.

Newsletters

Newsletters are a common way for consultants to promote themselves. It is a subtle form of advertising that can give you credibility, as well as providing advice to readers. Most newsletters are distributed free, since they are used as a marketing device. Once you establish a reputation and a large mailing list, economics and demand may justify charging a fee for a subscription.

The important features of a newsletter are effective use of colour and layout, a professional appearance, and well-written articles on interesting subjects. Most potential clients who will receive your newsletter are very busy; unless the newsletter captures the attention and is easily readable, it will not serve the purpose that you intend. The newsletter should have tips, news and ideas, and possibly a question and answer column. The length should be two to six pages on A4 paper, and published on a regular basis, such as monthly, bi-monthly, quarterly or half-yearly. The frequency of your publication will depend on your finances and time.

A newsletter is distributed in the same manner outlined earlier for brochures. When sending out brochures with covering letters in response to an enquiry, you should also include a recent copy of your newsletter. As in the case of direct mail marketing and brochures, you should address the newsletter to the key people in target organisations.

Use of a public relations consultant

PR consultants can be expensive but they can get your name into the media, place articles and generally publicise your activities. It might at least be worthwhile contacting a firm to see what it can offer.

Registration

Some professional associations such as the Institute of Management Consultants and the Institute of Personnel Management maintain lists of their members who wish to be placed on their register. Names are then passed on to enquirers of consultants on the register who have the appropriate skills. Registration is a 'bread on the water' approach which will not necessarily pay off, but it may be worth pursuing.

Chapter 6

Selling Your Consultancy Services

Your efforts at marketing have been successful. A prospective client has agreed to see you or you have been invited to tender for an assignment. In either case your task now is to sell your services. 'Selling' may sound unprofessional to some people, but consultancy is a business as well as a profession, and you have to sell to stay in business. There are many consultants who have lots of professional expertise and are good operators, but if they cannot sell work they will not survive long. And in the larger firms the ability to develop the practice, to sell and to earn fees will be key criteria for advancement. Professional skill is important but it is not enough.

The problem with selling consultancy is that you are selling an intangible product. Clearly, you will emphasise in your sales pitch the benefits that the prospective client will gain from retaining you. You will still have to convince him that you can deliver what you promise. Your credibility will depend partly on your track record (and a good CV is an important selling tool) but, ultimately, your success will depend on the impact you make on the client at your meeting and on the quality of your proposal.

'Hard' selling, however, is inappropriate and can be counter-productive. Clients expect a professional approach which calmly, quietly, clearly but persuasively convinces them that you understand the problem and will be able to help them solve it.

There are three ways in which you will meet clients:

1. *Exploratory meeting* when you are discussing generally with a client his affairs and problems and are giving him information about your services and yourself.
2. *Assignment meetings* when you have been invited to pitch or tender for a consultancy job.
3. *Surveys* when you carry out a lengthier and more detailed survey of a client's situation with a view to the production of a proposal.

Exploratory meetings

You will only be involved in an exploratory meeting if, for whatever reason, the prospective client has some problems which may need outside help and is also interested in what you have to offer. The problems which may not have been defined and the link between the problems and your role in solving them may not have been established.

Objectives

For meetings of this nature, indeed for any meeting, it is essential to have a clear idea of what your objectives are. These could be described as being to:

(a) find out as much about the client and his affairs as possible so that he reveals any concerns or apprehensions he may have about his business;

(b) tell him about your firm and yourself in a way which relates to his perceptions about his situation and the sort of help he needs;

(c) convince him that what you have to offer is what he needs;

(d) develop this general review, if possible, into a more specific discussion of a particular problem or set of problems and how you would help, ie narrowing down the broad assessment, and channelling the meeting into an area where you know you have relevant competencies;

(e) clinch the meeting, ideally with an offer of an assignment from the client, or at least having gained the opportunity to conduct a further assignment or survey with a view to preparing a proposal.

Achieving the objective

To achieve these objectives it is necessary to:

(a) find out as much about the client as you can beforehand – accounts, press references, articles, Dun and Bradstreet reports etc;

(b) get the client to talk about his problems first, choosing the right moment to interject with comments which indicate that you are with him and also, subtly, point the way to what you can do;

(c) ask intelligent and perceptive questions – prepare a checklist in advance, but don't refer to it in the meeting – you want to appear spontaneous;

(d) avoid indulging in lengthy or over-prepared sales pitches about your firm and your consultancy products – this is what is meant by not going in for the hard sell; but

(e) seize any opportunities you can to relate what you have to offer to the client's own assessment of his needs;

(f) quote wherever you can brief and pointed examples of what you have achieved and how clients have benefited from your services;

(g) ensure that at the right moment the client gets an overview about your firm and your track record – present your brochure;

(h) if possible, clinch the meeting with a positive agreement about how you might help – perhaps to be explored more thoroughly at a further meeting;

(i) if you cannot clinch the meeting, at least leave the door open for future contacts.

Assignment meetings

During the meeting

The day has now arrived. You made certain you were at the client's office 10 to 15 minutes prior to the appointment to relax and compose yourself. You are feeling self-confident and positive about the meeting because you have prepared yourself thoroughly and worked through in your own mind a role-play of events that are soon to occur.

Arriving early gives you an opportunity to observe the dynamics of the office and personnel, and the general tone of the company. If you are going to have a relationship with a client, these simple factors are important to know beforehand.

When the meeting starts, it is important to shake hands with a firm grasp. A less than firm grasp will betray an insecure personality or lack of confidence in your abilities, and that impression alone could lose a project. It is important to project consciously a confident personality, a positive attitude, a firm method of speaking, and an attentive and relaxed stance. Exhibit a sense of control and leadership. A client wants to associate with a person who projects himself or herself well.

During the meeting, you should spend almost all the time asking questions and little time answering them. After the initial social pleasantries and after you have briefly exchanged backgrounds, control the meeting by asking your prepared questions. It is helpful to advise the client that you will be taking notes as this is a fact-finding interview. Having a prepared checklist is evidence of efficient administration and an assurance that no questions will be overlooked and interview consistency will be maintained.

Ask for examples to illustrate general statements. Ask open-ended as well as very specific questions, and let the client do the talking. If a pause occurs, be prepared with the next question or other appropriate reaction. Listen intently to what the client says and how the client perceives the problem. If you want the client to continue elaborating on a situation, use questions starting with how, why, who, what or where or state, 'That's interesting, can you tell me more about that?'

Be aware of non-verbal communication in body posture, mannerisms, voice patterns and behaviour. When forming an impression of a client's situation or opinion, restate it back to the client for confirmation.

If a client attempts to ask you a lot of questions, try to deflect the line of questioning back to the client. If the client asks specific questions about how you think the problem can be dealt with, or the various steps or stages that should be considered, don't answer the questions directly. Your first interview is a fact-finding stage and you should not become involved in speculation or offering advice. Tell the client that you will certainly give an opinion later, after you have had an opportunity to review and analyse the facts and assess the options. Say that it would be premature and unprofessional for you to provide an opinion at this early stage. You don't want to give away free consulting, especially based on incomplete information.

Try to avoid committing yourself on fees or total costs at this stage. You need time after the meeting to define the programme of work required and to decide on the consultancy resources you will need.

Try to understand and anticipate client fears or concerns in advance and deal with them. A client may have underlying biases about you as a consultant that could affect the interview and its outcome. By knowing in advance the fears that might exist, you can counter them directly during the interview and proposal stages. Studies have shown that the following anxieties often exist. They are listed generally in order of priority.

- A consultant may be incompetent.
- The client may be continually dependent upon the consultant once the first relationship begins.
- The consultant might assume or interfere with managerial control during the project.
- The consultant's fees are excessive relative to the services provided.
- The consultant may not be able to complete the project in time.
- The need for a consultant is an admission of failure on the part of management.

- The consultant might disclose confidential internal information.
- The consultant might have inaccurately analysed the needs and therefore will give an improper diagnosis.
- The consultant will lack impartiality.
- Colleagues and staff may react adversely to the use of a consultant.

Normally, a consultant will meet a client in the client's office. The client feels comfortable in familiar surroundings and is therefore more relaxed. The advantage to the consultant is having the opportunity to view the client's offices and operations, and to leave diplomatically if the meeting is unproductive or continues too long.

Try not to have a meeting just before lunch, as the client could have a lunch commitment or be distracted by the time or feel hungry.

Attempt to arrange an appointment for the time when you are at your peak of mental clarity so that you will create the most positive impression.

Make sure you arrive on time. Being late automatically creates a negative impression and can destroy the client's desire to deal with you. A small matter such as being late for an important appointment could represent an attitude and management style, which could cause conflict during the consulting project.

At the end of the interview, ask the client if he or she would like to see a proposal and whether it should be a simple or a detailed one.

Throughout the interview, be aware of the fears and concerns that might be present. Try to make sure you have dealt with all of them to the client's satisfaction.

The following is a checklist of points you should cover during the meeting.

Assignment meeting checklist

Problem or need definition
It is essential to get a clear and realistic definition of the problem or need.

1. Has the client defined the problem or need in writing?
2. Have formal terms of reference been issued by the client?
3. If the answer to questions 1 or 2 is no, what is the overall problem or need as perceived by the client?
4. What challenges or opportunities are faced by the client?
5. Can the problem or need as defined above be analysed into constituent parts, each of which might form a segment of the assignment?

Problem or need context

The consultant must understand the context in which the problem or need exists.

6. What business is the client in?
7. What is the strategy for the future?
8. What are the strengths and weaknesses of the enterprise or organisation?
9. What, in general, are the opportunities and threats facing the client?
10. How does the immediate problem or need fit into the context defined at questions 6-9 above?
11. What solutions, if any, have been attempted in the past?
12. Who attempted to solve the problem and with what results?
13. If the attempt was unsuccessful, why did it fail? (The assignment may be impractical or impossible to complete to the client's satisfaction.)
14. What initial steps towards a solution does the client have in mind?
15. What needs to be done to ensure that the solution wins wide acceptance? (See also questions 16-22 below.)

Attitudes of management, staff and the trade unions

The success of an assignment frequently depends upon the attitudes of the client's employees and unions.

16. To what extent has the problem or need been identified by top management?
17. Will top management actively support the assignment?
18. What are the views of senior and middle management and supervision? To what extent will each category be supportive?
19. What reactions are likely from employees?
20. Are the people affected ready for change?
21. If not, what problems are likely to arise in managing change? If so:
22. Are staff unionised? If so:
    (a) to what extent?
    (b) what is the likely reaction of the union(s)?
    (c) could there be conflict between management and the union(s) over this project? If so:
    (d) How might the conflict be resolved?
    (e) are trade unions likely to be involved in the project? If so, how?

Benefits
It is necessary to check that the client's expectations are specific, realistic, measurable and attainable.

23. What specific benefits must be obtained for the client to be satisfied?

Assignment data
Information needs to be obtained on how the assignment is to be conducted.

24. What is the time limit for completing the assignment as specified by the client?
25. Is the specified time limit realistic?
26. What resources (skills and number of consultants) is the consultant likely to need?
27. Are the resources available to complete the assignment satisfactorily within the agreed time scale?
28. What arrangement will the client make to provide staff and other facilities (eg, office space, typing, photocopying, fax facilities) for the consultant?
29. To whom will the consultant report?
30. Will there be a steering group?
31. Will the consultant be part of an existing project team? Or will a project team need to be set up?
32. What will be the consultant's role in the project team? Who will lead it?
33. Will the consultant have access to the information needed to carry out the assignment?
34. How much travel will be involved?
35. What arrangements for progress or 'milestone' meetings should be made?
36. Should the consultant produce interim reports? If so, in what form?
37. What type of final report does the client want?
38. Is the client likely to want help in implementation?

Fees and costs
Try and obtain, directly or indirectly, some idea of fee arrangements and how much the client is prepared to pay to assist in costing the proposal.

39. What type of fee arrangement is preferred by the client?
40. How much is the client prepared to spend on the project?

41. How comfortable is the client with any preliminary indications from the consultant on fee rates and total costs? (It is normally inadvisable at this stage to be too specific about costs.)

Overall conclusions

42. Is the consultant comfortable that a clear understanding of the client's real problem or need exists?
43. Has the client been convinced that the consultant is qualified to carry out the assignment?
44. Is the consultant convinced that he or she is qualified to conduct the assignment and will meet the client's needs?

Once the meeting is over, you should review the data while it is still fresh in your mind. Identify the problems as you see them and analyse the needs. Then outline the possible solutions and draft a proposal. The proposal steps are outlined in the next chapter.

The normal steps that follow include writing a thank-you letter to the client as soon as possible after the meeting and saying a proposal will follow as soon as it is complete.

Why you should turn down business

After your meeting and assessment of the client and project and other factors involved, you may decide that it would be wise not to accept the project. That decision takes insight and foresight, and many consultants find it difficult to make. Consultants may be influenced by factors such as the need for cash flow, seeing a challenge in the project, seeing potential marketing opportunities, desiring some form of activity because of the lack of it, or wanting to help because a client is in need. Some of the reasons you should consider turning down business are as follows:

(a) A client looks as though he or she is on the verge of business failure. (The various reasons for business failure include management incompetence, imbalanced experience, lack of management experience, or lack of experience in the product or service line. Some of the danger signals may include: lack of a business plan, high overhead costs, low morale, lack of cash flow, lack of understanding of financial information, indecisiveness, backlog of commitments, inefficiency, poor communication and general chaos. As a consequence, you do not want to be burdened with the stress of a client failure or the risk of not collecting your fee.)
(b) The client has a reputation for paying late or not at all.

(c) The client has a bad reputation for other reasons, and you do not want to be associated with that client.

(d) You do not like the client personally.

(e) A proposed project is illegal or unpleasant.

(f) You are over-committed with other projects and unable to accept the work and perform satisfactorily and on time.

(g) The project may be a 'poisoned chalice', ie the consultant may be faced with insuperable problems outside his control such as office politics, hostility from managers, staff or unions, or a client who is not prepared to give adequate support.

(h) The potential job is too small for your time, priorities or cash flow.

(i) The potential job is too large for your ability or desire to administer it.

(j) You lack the expertise to perform the job to the standard that would be required.

(k) The client wants to pay you less than you feel is fair to complete the project.

(l) The project would involve you compromising what you consider to be your professional and ethical standards.

(m) The client does not appear to appreciate your skills and abilities fully.

(n) The client does not have the finance needed to complete the assignment.

How to turn down unwanted business

Once you have decided that you do not want the business at all, or in the form that is available, there are various tactics and techniques involved in turning down the business so as to maintain goodwill and not hurt the client's feelings.

If the proposed project is simply unsuitable for you, you may wish to turn it down completely. There are different ways of rejecting projects directly:

(a) Tell the client that your present workload is very heavy and unfortunately you are unable to accept the job. This option makes you appear more attractive and desirable to the client for possible future projects.

(b) Tell the client you are unable to comply technically with the job specifications. This typically occurs with government agencies. If you are expected to take a government job because of previous projects, and you want to be considered favourably in the future, you could propose an approach that you feel the client will reject as it may be outside the stated or unstated guidelines.

(c) Tell the client that you do not perform the particular type of service being requested, either because you do not have the capacity, or it isn't your current field. If you normally perform that type of consulting, state that at the present time you are directing your talents and priorities in a slightly different direction.

(d) Bid the job too high. You can quote a fee much higher than you think the job is worth or that other competitors might bid. The risk here, of course, is that your bid might be accepted.

There may be occasions when you would accept a job if it was changed to meet your needs. Some of the techniques you could consider include:

(a) Accept only part of the proposed project. You could encourage other consultants to accept parts of the project you do not wish to handle.

(b) Redefine the project to meet your needs, and offer to conduct the assignment on your own terms. This approach only works if the client's goals, objectives and expectations can be met without additional costs.

(c) Accept the job but act as project manager and employ other consultants to assist you in completing the job.

Surveys

Surveys are carried out when it is necessary to get more information about the client's circumstances and requirements than would be possible in a meeting lasting an hour or two. A survey is therefore a data collection process which might mean examining records, reports and printouts, but could also involve interviewing a number of members of the client's staff to obtain information and views from them about the problem.

A survey can last anything from a day to a week or more. It is quite common for clients to pay fees for a survey and, unless you are certain that you will get the assignment and so be able to recover your survey costs, it is advisable to raise the question of fees. Turn down invitations to do prolonged surveys unless you are paid to do them.

Chapter 7

Consulting Proposals

Most initial meetings result in a request for a proposal. The proposal plays a significant role in your ability to obtain consulting assignments. This chapter covers some of the basic concepts and tactics required to succeed in your proposal.

What is a proposal?

A proposal is a letter or document that you prepare for a client describing in the first place your understanding of the client's needs. This is very important as your client, to have confidence in you, must be satisfied that you understand the problem as well as the client does. It also states what you intend to do for the client, and indicates in specific terms the anticipated results and potential benefits.

A proposal is a selling document. It is intended to be informative and appealing and to persuade the client to contract for your services.

Private versus public sector proposals

Public sector proposals tend to be more formal than private sector proposals. When a client requests a proposal, the request is made on the assumption that anyone offering goods or services is properly qualified and equipped to do so. The government requires that you demonstrate your own competence and prove that your facilities, experience, resources and whatever else are adequate to handle the requirements. The client is evaluating not only the merits of the programme you propose versus the merits of competitive programmes, but also your credentials versus the credentials of your competitors. It is common for government agencies to require that you outline your personal qualifications. One reason government agencies request such information is that they are required by procurement regulations to make an objective evaluation of each proposal. Your qualifications provide one specific comparison.

Government departments/agencies have various evaluation factors.

An example of the criteria a government agency might use is shown in Appendix 2.

Private sector proposals can be far more flexible in their selection requirements. Therefore, pragmatism and subjective factors have more of an influence on the final decision.

Solicited versus unsolicited proposals

Solicited proposals are those requests that are made by a prospective client from the public or private sector. An organisation requesting a proposal has already identified some needs. Your proposal will be judged on its quality, timeliness, reliability and effectiveness.

An unsolicited proposal is designed by a consultant who perceives a need and is confident that it can be met through the use of the consultant's services.

Solicited proposals generally involve a competition between two or more consultants who pitch for the project. With an unsolicited proposal, you may be the only person being considered.

Simple and formal proposals

Simple proposal
The simple proposal is a written statement that includes the following items:

(a) A definition of the problem to be dealt with (terms of reference).
(b) A description of the work to be done.
(c) The name of the consultant performing the work.
(d) The services or personnel to be provided by the client.
(e) The date work will begin and the length of time required to complete the assignment.
(f) An outline of anticipated categories of costs to be paid by the client.
(g) The fees to be paid for services rendered and the terms arranged.

The proposal is signed by the consultant and if agreed, the client signs a copy of the proposal or letter. The letter of proposal and agreement constitutes a legal contract and is similar to a letter of agreement.

Formal proposal
A formal proposal is considerably more detailed in that all aspects of the

project are spelled out in full. It is similar to a formal contract and offers protections to both the consultant and the client.

The proposal does not become a legally binding contract until the client agrees and signs the proposal document to that effect, or a covering letter referring to the proposal as a binding contract is signed, or a formal contract is drafted reflecting the contents of the proposal and signed by both parties.

The basic proposal

A basic formal proposal might contain the following sections:

1. Introduction
The introduction simply says that this is a proposal on how you could assist with a named product and that the proposal is set out under the following headings.

2. Understanding of the situation
A section which explains your understanding of the situation – the problem to be solved or the opportunity to be pursued.

3. Terms of reference
A definition of the terms of reference for an assignment to deal with the matters discussed in 2. above.

4. Programme of work
A description of the programme of work required to meet the terms of reference. Wherever appropriate, this would be broken down into defined stages to facilitate programme planning and control and to convey to the client that you will be adopting a logical and systematic approach. This is a key part of the proposal in which you have the best opportunity to demonstrate that you adopt a professional approach to problem-solving and that you know your business when it comes to designing programmes and, by implication, completing them satisfactorily.

5. Timetable
A definition of the starting and finishing times of each section of the programme and an indication of the total elapsed time to complete the engagement. The need for and positioning of progress or 'milestone' meetings might be referred to.

6. Staffing

A description of the staff resources that you will assign to the project. This section might also mention the use of the client's staff.

7. Fees and costs

A statement of your fee rates for each grade of consultant you would use on the project. An estimate of the total cost of fees is also usually given, based on the fee rate and the number of consultant days required to complete the assignment as described in the proposal.

8. Conclusion

The conclusion sets out the benefits the assignment will bring to the client and underlines your eagerness and capacity to carry it out. It should also state that you are willing to provide any additional information that may be required.

9. Appendices

The appendices might include:

(a) a brief description of your firm;
(b) the programme and timetable expressed as a bar chart;
(c) CVs of yourself and/or any other consultants who will take part in the engagement;
(d) your standard terms and conditions;
(e) any other supporting data.

This basic proposal provides a format which would be effective on many occasions. But it can be elaborated on, as described in the next section.

Detailed proposal format

Guidelines for a successful proposal

The basis for your written contract will be the matters that you discuss at the proposal stage. Make sure you expand on the need, outcome, benefits and results. Do not expand too much on the process or methods. This protects you from a client rejecting the proposal, and performing the project in-house using your proposal as a guide or submitting your proposal to other consultants for estimates and then hiring someone else who uses the process you detailed.

Also keep in mind when you are preparing the proposal that your client might have some of the concerns and fears outlined in the preceding chapter. Try to minimise any concerns in the content of your proposal.

You should consider having a number of standardised proposals if there is a similarity in the type of services you offer. If the standardised documents are on a word processor, they can easily be adapted to include or exclude paragraphs and to make the document an original. It is also very easy to revise a document on a word processor. The standardised proposal contains all the basics of any proposal, leaving open those items that are specific to each project. Another advantage of a standardised proposal is your ability to deliver the completed proposal to the client shortly after your initial meeting.

The sample proposal format and guidelines (Figure 7.1) is rather formal and detailed. It may include clauses that are not applicable or appropriate in all situations, as each project is unique.

Figure 7.1 *Proposal format*

---

1. **Table of contents:** This includes headings and page numbers.

2. **Introduction:** It is important to persuade the client that you understand the project and the underlying factors that influence it. Briefly outline and analyse the factors that demonstrate the need. State that the matter is important and warrants professional outside assistance. Emphasise that you want to help and that you are the most appropriate source of help.

3. **Project purpose:** The purpose and goals of the engagement are outlined here clearly and accurately. State the purpose and goals in the client's own words so that the client can identify with the proposal. During your initial interview you attempted to elicit from the client what the client perceived as being the needs or problems and the means of resolving them. Detail the goals in such a way that you can refer to them as specific and measurable outcomes to have a reference point for measuring the progress of the project and satisfying the client.

4. **Terms of reference:** It is often useful to state formally the terms of reference for the assignment. This summarises and confirms the project purpose definition and also provides a formal basis for assessing the success of the assignment.

5. **Project benefits:** Highlight the anticipated benefits the client will receive. Do not promise results you cannot guarantee, but the client has to be given some realistic hope of success. This is a particularly important section as the client has to understand and recognise the benefits in order to justify the financial and administrative commitment. Your client may have to account to other directors or shareholders. The more detail you provide, the more you are assisting your client to assist you.

6. **Approach, scope and plan:** Compare and contrast several possible approaches to the project, if appropriate. Explain how you will proceed

---

in general terms. Define the scope and limits of the proposed consulting service. Divide the tasks into smaller segments that provide clear stages in the project as reference points for you and your client. As mentioned earlier, provide sufficient information to demonstrate your competence, but not enough about the process and techniques to provide a formula for the client to perform the project without you.

7. **Project schedule:** Draw up a schedule which lists the specific tasks required to meet the terms of reference. State the timing and sequence of tasks according to the various stages. A bar chart or functional flow diagram might help graphically to assist the client's understanding and provide a reference point for progress.

8. **Progress reports:** It is important to maintain continual communication with the client. As explained in earlier chapters, the more information you provide for your client, the more confidence the client will have in you, and the less risk there is of problems occurring. Progress reports are frequently made at specific stages, when interim invoices are sent. A client is more disposed to pay if tangible benefits can be seen and specific problems have been resolved. The frequency and format of periodic progress reports should be specified.

9. **Costing summary:** Explain your fees, types of fee arrangement, invoicing procedures, and timing of bills. Provide an estimate of the total cost of fees based on the estimated number of consultant days or hours required and the daily or hourly fee rate. Chapter 8 deals with setting fee rates and other aspects of pricing for consultancy assignments. Detail the expected expenses that will be passed on directly to the client. Your client should understand that your estimate for time and costs is an estimate only. Provide sufficient detail about your fees, so that your client appreciates the correlation between the amount of time expended and the cost of your services. Outline any other terms and conditions or variables that could affect the final cost.

10. **Personnel and qualifications:** Provide a brief background history of your firm and the personnel who will be consulting on the project. If you have had experience solving problems similar to the client's, make reference to that. Select only those aspects of your background experience that relate directly to the client and the proposal.

11. **Subcontracts:** If you are subcontracting or collaborating with other consultants, it is important to specify who they are and what duties they will perform. Specify whether you or the client is responsible for their technical performance to avoid any future problems.

12. **Use of client personnel:** It is important that the client understands what commitments and obligations will be his or her responsibility. If you are to delegate responsibilities or otherwise receive assistance from the client's staff or executives, you should make it clear that your fee

estimate is based on the use of client personnel. Specify personnel duties and time required if possible.

13. **Senior management support:** Make the executives aware that their support is vital to the success of the project. It is important that support for the project is communicated throughout the organisation to gain cooperation and compliance. If regular meetings are going to be held with senior executives, specify the purpose and frequency of such meetings.

14. **Steering committee function, if applicable:** A steering committee reviews, coordinates, assists and implements the consultant's work. It provides momentum and organisational credibility and decision-making functions for the project. Detail the purposes, composition and responsibilities of this committee.

15. **Output material included:** Describe any reports, surveys, instructional material or other products that are part of the proposal.

16. **Management plan:** Describe your approach to managing the overall project. Who will be the client contact person, and what will his or her management role and authority be pertaining to the project?

17. **Disclaimers:** If you have used disclaimers regarding the project, make sure that the reason is outlined. Your role is strictly that of an adviser, not a decision-maker, and any benefit achieved is based on both your recommendations and the client's actions and decisions. If your client does not fulfil his or her obligations and support, your responsibility and choices should be outlined. Indicate who has ownership and control over any proprietary information that could develop from your services; for example, instructional material.

18. **References:** If requested, or if it is your style and wish to provide client references, make sure that you obtain written permission in advance from the references. Update them to make sure they still think highly of you.

19. **Summary and closing of proposal:** This should be a short restatement of your belief in the importance of the engagement. Mention your availability to answer questions. If you are prepared to begin the project within a short time after the client's acceptance, state that clearly. You want to stimulate the client's need and persuade the client that you can fulfil the need.

A checklist used by a public sector organisation to evaluate proposals is given in Appendix 2.

Presenting your proposal

How you package your proposal is nearly as important as how it is stated.

If possible, your proposal should be prepared on a word processor, as that reflects professionalism and quality secretarial resources.

A covering letter should accompany your proposal thanking your client for the time and cooperation during the meeting and for the opportunity to submit a proposal. Highlight the topics discussed and state that you can help because you have had experience with this type of problem and would like to have the opportunity to be of service. Offer to answer any questions either by phone or at an arranged meeting. State that you will phone within 10 working days to discuss the proposal further. Put that date in your diary. If you have not heard from the client within that period, make sure that you contact the client on the tenth day.

You may wish to suggest in your covering letter, if you didn't mention it in the proposal, that references are available on request. You may wish to suggest that the client contact some of your other clients to discuss work you have performed. This should demonstrate your self-confidence and increase the client's trust and confidence in you.

Proposal follow-up

Your client may be slow in responding to your proposal. You do not want to appear to be pressuring the client, but you may have to take certain steps to clarify the situation or obtain a contract.

You stated in your covering letter that you would contact the client within 10 working days. It is appropriate, then, that you do contact the client on the tenth day to answer any questions. You may receive further questions at that point, or obtain a positive or negative response to your proposal.

If the reason for the delay appears inexplicable, you may wish to wait for a further five working days and then drop in to see the client in person to ask if a decision has been made. This approach may or may not be appropriate in a given situation.

If a client is waiting for a committee decision, find out when the committee will meet to discuss the proposal and follow up by phone to the client the following day. You may also wish to consider giving an acceptance time limit in your proposal to encourage prompt consideration. In a given situation you might adopt the attitude that you would like to know one way or the other within a certain time. The client could construe the acceptance time in a positive fashion, as it could imply that you are in demand and have other projects available to you that require a decision.

What to do if your proposal is not accepted

It is helpful if you can discover why you received a rejection. It may not be appropriate, practical or possible for you to obtain the answer from the client. Budget restraints, other priorities or lack of consensus could be reasons. Another consultant may have been awarded the contract. If possible, find out who obtained the assignment and why that proposal was selected in preference to your own. Rejected proposals can provide a good learning experience.

Regardless of the circumstances, write a thank-you letter to the client expressing your appreciation for his or her time, interest and cooperation, and mention that you would be pleased to submit a proposal for consideration in any future projects.

How to avoid giving away free consulting

At this stage you should know whether your proposal was rejected or accepted. If it was rejected, you may have provided too much information in your proposal to your client, who in turn used the information for his or her benefit. In other words, you gave away free consulting. If your proposal was accepted, and you now have a contract or a contract is being prepared, you should be aware of the various ways that clients can innocently or intentionally obtain your advice for free.

At times, you may decide to share your knowledge and ideas in an attempt to build goodwill with the client or prospective client. That is a judgement you will have to make at the time. But you are running a business, which requires income and profit. You cannot carelessly give away the only product you have, which is time and skill.

Potential client interview or discussion

A potential client may contact you and wish to discuss ideas and problems with you on the telephone, over lunch or at the client's office or your office. The potential client (referred to as 'client' for convenience) wants to 'pick your brains'. You willingly cooperate because of your desire to obtain a consulting assignment.

The strategic solution is to confirm that you do provide service in the area concerned and you are available to the client on a professional basis and would be pleased to establish a relationship. Answer any concerns raised by the client by asking questions aimed at drawing out information. Do not offer solutions but imply that there are solutions to the problems discussed.

If answers are specifically requested, respond that you require more information before providing an answer. State that it would be unprofessional for you to provide an opinion without sufficient information on which to base that opinion. Again, restate that you would be pleased to discuss the matter further on a professional basis if so wished.

These deflective techniques are the same ones outlined in the preceding chapter relating to the assignment meeting. Ask the client directly if he or she is interested in retaining a consultant to provide assistance in the specific area of concern. Clarify if the client would like you to submit a proposal to resolve the problem. Decide if the client is a serious enough prospect to spend the time on a proposal.

Make it clear throughout the discussion that you are paid for professional services and that you are capable of assisting the client on a fee for service basis.

Client need analysis
A client might perceive that a problem exists, but not understand the precise nature of the problem. The client implies to you that if an analysis of the needs is made with recommendations for resolution an attractive contract could immediately result. This teaser can entice unsophisticated or new consultants to provide a thorough diagnosis without fee.

A naive consultant can be easily exploited by this technique. The risk, of course, is that no subsequent contracts materialise or some other consultant is retained. One way of resolving this problem is to recommend that the client enter into a contract with the first stage to be a diagnostic stage. After the diagnosis is made, with recommendations, the consultant could proceed to the next stage of contract and implement the recommendations. That way the consultant is protected by contract, and the sincerity of the client is assured.

An option can be inserted in the contract that if the client elects not to proceed with the recommendation, the consultant is assured payment of an agreed sum in consideration for the time and energy expended during the diagnostic phase.

Free detailed advice in the written proposal
In your proposal you may write a complete, detailed formula with all the necessary instructions together with an outline of the methods and steps required to attain the objective. The client now has the prescription for resolving the problem and can give it to other consultants to submit an estimate or implement the detailed proposal with in-house personnel.

One approach to avoid this problem is to write the proposal highlighting in detail the need that exists, the objectives that must be achieved in order to resolve the client's problem and the measurable, specific outcomes and benefits that will be attained at specific stages of the assignment.

A functional flow diagram graphically illustrating the steps is an effect-ive marketing tool. Play down or omit information on the processes or methods to be used.

Potential future benefit

A client may try to convince you that some future benefit, such as good-will or contacts, could occur if you performed the service. The condition is that you provide the service for free or a reduced amount as the price to pay for future opportunities and contacts.

This technique is normally exercised by larger or more influential clients who take advantage of a consultant's impressionable, desperate or opportunist nature. The client may attempt to blame the lack of financial recompense on budget allocations already spent, internal financial restraints being imposed or a general hold on all project commitments. From a consultant's viewpoint, the mere association with an influential or prestigious client could be an inducement.

As long as you are aware of the business and psychological dynamics at work, you can make a responsible, pragmatic decision. The decision might be to accede to the client's overtures, resist them or attempt to negotiate a more realistic package.

Additions to the original fixed price contract

You may be asked to perform additional work outside the original con-tract terms.

It is not uncommon for a client to request additional work, as all needs cannot be foreseen in advance or changing circumstances alter the needs. Once you are aware that the request is outside the fixed price contract terms, you should contact the client, draw this fact to the client's atten-tion in a polite fashion and suggest that a modified contract or addendum be negotiated to incorporate the additional work. You should then negotiate the amount and method of payment for the additional work.

This situation reinforces the importance of being specific in a fixed price contract as to the services that are to be performed. Ambiguity in terms could lead to a difference of opinion, an impasse, legal problems and loss of goodwill as well as loss of a client.

Depending on the circumstances, a formal contract amendment may not be required; a confirmation letter outlining the amendments and signed by both parties may be enough. The method is a matter of style, nature of client and other circumstances.

Free consulting in a follow-up situation

You can run into problems if you have performed your services as outlined in your contract, but the client continues to need your services for operating the project. For example, suppose you recommended a type of computer hardware that was subsequently installed on the client's premises, and the client's personnel had difficulty learning how to operate the new equipment. You might feel an obligation to assist the client by giving the necessary explanations to the personnel. You may then be continually phoned by the client asking you to return to explain various features. Unless you are aware of the process occurring, you could be providing a considerable amount of free consulting.

The obvious solution is to anticipate the situation in advance and incorporate provisions for follow-up consultation fees into the original contract. The contract can specify the method of payment and terms. One option is a time retainer contract, which means that you perform a specified service regularly, (eg, several specified hours or days per month). Another option is an availability retainer contract. This means you are 'on call' for a fixed monthly fee as outlined in the terms of the agreement.

Relatives, associates and friends

Relatives and friends may frequently come to you for advice. You must develop ways to maintain the relationship but clarify your role as a professional who provides service for a fee.

You can develop various subtle but effective approaches. One technique is to say that you have a policy of not advising family or friends because of possible conflict of interest or bias. Because you value the relationship and operate by professional standards, you feel it would not be appropriate or responsible or you would prefer not to provide professional advice that they might rely on.

Another approach is to say you are unable to provide advice because of incomplete information, and that it would be irresponsible, unprofessional and unfair on your part to give an opinion based on incomplete facts.

You have choices. You can either decline to provide advice, provide advice for free or establish your relationship in the context as a business one and negotiate a fee for service. It is also helpful to keep in mind that you can be exposed to professional liability and negligent claims if your advice is followed and problems occur even though you did not charge or get paid for your advice.

Chapter 8

Fees and Estimates

Setting fees

The fees you are able to set – your fee structure – will be governed by the market-place. There are two markets:

1. General market rates – the fees that different parts of the public and private sectors are prepared to pay for different types of consultancy services.
2. Individual market rates – the fees that can be charged by or for the individual consultant depending on his or her field of expertise, experience, qualifications and reputation.

General market rates
By whatever means possible you must get a 'feel' for market rates. Ask people you know who engage consultants, ask other consultants. Find out, if you can, what the big firms are charging in different sectors. You may discover that rates vary from sector to sector. Public sector organisations attempt to get away with lower fees and often succeed. The rates for international assignments may be different from those in the UK – greater or less depending on where they are.

Your market rate survey will show a wide range of rates. In 1989 large firms are charging out their junior consultants at £500 a day, their senior consultants at £600 to £750 a day, their managing consultants at £750 to £1000 a day and their directors and partners at £1000-plus a day.

Sole practitioners and small firms generally charge out at a lower rate – the range in 1989 for established and professional consultants being from £300 to £1000 a day. There are, however, amateurs, moonlighters, part-timers and desperate redundant executives who try to undercut the market with fees of as little as £100 a day. And there are some exceptional people who can charge more than £1000 a day.

All these rates are subject to variation according to sector and location.

Fee rates in London and the prosperous parts of the UK are often higher than elsewhere.

Individual market rates

The rates charged by sole practitioners mentioned above do, of course, vary with the marketability of the individual consultant. Tyros might find it difficult to charge much more than £350 a day, unless they have had exceptionally relevant experience in their jobs prior to taking up consultancy, or enjoy a well-established reputation. Fully experienced consultants may well charge from £500 to £750 and upwards a day. (These are all 1989 figures.)

What rate should you charge?

If you are a moonlighter or someone making a bit on the side you might be happy to charge as little as £100 a day. But if you are trying to make a reasonably good living out of consultancy you must aim higher than that. Remember that many people really believe that they only get what they pay for. Your credibility as a consultant may well be related to the value you place on your services.

If you are a sole practitioner clients will normally expect you to charge lower fees than a large firm would for consultants with broadly equivalent experience and capabilities. Such clients will say that you don't have to carry the overheads of a large firm, although this could be a fallacious argument – there is such a thing as economies of scale. Perhaps more reasonably, they will claim that a large firm has back-up resources and access to databanks that you lack. The counter-argument that the quality of an assignment depends on the quality of the consultant and that you are providing a high-quality personal service does not always convince clients. It may well be the case that the sole practitioner can do as good a job, if not a better one, than a consultant from a large firm, but you may have to accept, reluctantly but gracefully, that you will be expected to charge less.

Clearly, although fees are largely market driven, you have still to charge at a rate which, based on assumptions about the proportion of your time you will be able to charge out (your utilisation rate), will provide you with the return on your investment of time, energy and expertise and the standard of living that you want.

It will help you to make decisions on fees if you draw up a break-even chart as illustrated in Figure 8.1. This indicates the revenues and break-even points you will achieve for different levels of fees and utilisation rates. In this example it is assumed that the consultant:

(a) is a sole practitioner working from home using the minimum of secretarial help and able to keep non-recoverable expenses down to £12,000 a year;

(b) needs to draw at least £25,000 a year from the practice to live on (a + b is the break-even point of £37,000);

(c) has 220 days of chargeable time available; this is calculated by deducting from the total of 260 working days in the year, 25 days' personal holiday, 8 public holidays, and 7 days for illness and conferences: 40 in all.

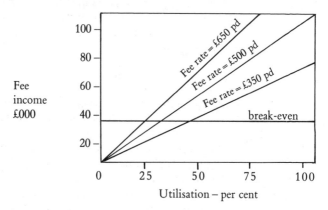

Figure 8.1. *Break-even chart*

Varying fees

You should consider adopting a range of fee rates. The minimum rate could be fixed by break-even point analysis and an estimate of your market value in sectors where market rates for consultancy are low. The maximum rate could also be fixed by reference to the top market rate for your skills. You might, for example, wish to adopt a standard rate of £500 a day and be prepared to flex it between £350 and £650 depending on your assessment of the market, the client and your worth in a particular situation. You would have to be careful to be consistent in your charging practices with the same clients or with clients in a sector where information about fees might be exchanged.

Consultants sometimes charge less for long assignments where the work is guaranteed. This could be beneficial as long as the reduced fee rate is above your break-even point. Clients may ask for 'quantity discounts'. If this is a possibility, it is best to discuss terms in advance before committing yourself in a proposal. You want to avoid haggling afterwards.

Increasing fees

From time to time you will want to increase your fees. This could be based on your regular monthly, quarterly or other review of your cash flow statements, profit and loss statements or projected needs. Your utilisation rate is also a factor.

If you are considering increasing fees, it is tactically a good idea to do it at a fixed time every year, such as 1 January. You should also attempt to notify your clients at least three months in advance, in writing, of your intention to increase your fees. Include a brief explanation about the reasons, such as an increase in costs, if appropriate. Invite the client to contact you if there are any questions. It is important, for obvious reasons, to keep the increase competitive.

Daily or hourly rate?

It is quite common to quote a daily rate, although there may be situations where you are giving intermittent services or advice or regularly working long hours where an hourly rate is more appropriate. If you assume a seven-hour working day, excluding luncheon, your hourly rate is one-seventh of your daily rate. You might want to round this up to take account of lack of continuity.

A daily rate suggests that if you are working full time for a client you charge no more if you work longer than your normal hours. You will be expected to work client hours and, indeed, should do so if the client is within easy reach of your base. In fact, you might find yourself working late with the client's executives. You should take this into account when setting your daily rate and decide to charge accordingly. Even when you are visiting clients for a day's work away from your base you will still be expected to travel mainly in your own time and get to the office or factory not much later than their normal starting time.

Travelling time

You should always state in your contract that you will charge for travelling time during the assignment, and this is quite reasonable if the job involves travelling away from your base. If, for example, you are visiting a number of sites during a day, you count that as a full day's work and in effect charge for any travelling time between units. You would not normally be expected to charge extra for travelling time when you are working full time locally. But it would be proper to allow for the time travelling to and from the client if you are engaged for part of a day.

Expenses

Your contract should state that expenses necessarily incurred during the assignment will be charged at cost. These can include travelling, overnight accommodation, subsistence, long-distance telephone calls, printing, duplicating, computing, the preparation of manuals and training material and large-scale typing. You would not normally be expected to charge for local calls or small-scale typing (letters, memoranda and brief reports).

You can reasonably charge for at least three-star hotels (eg Post Houses), first-class rail travel and club-class travel on overseas flights, but it might be advisable to clear the latter in advance with your clients. They cannot object if you are incurring expenses at the level they would expect to allow for their equivalent executives. Charge mileage according to the AA scale for your car.

Clients may request an estimate of your expenses in advance. If possible, avoid giving too firm an estimate. Circumstances might arise in which extra expenses are necessarily incurred and you want to be able to recover them.

Clients may ask you for evidence that the expenses have been incurred so you should keep a record of them and save receipts.

Estimating

One of the most critical but also the most tricky job a consultant has to do is to estimate the time required to complete the assignment, leading to the preparation of a total cost estimate. You do not necessarily have to provide your clients with a total cost and there are obvious dangers in working on a fixed-cost basis. Your time estimate may have been too modest or you may run into unforeseen snags which cause an overrun. In these circumstances, if you cannot get your client to agree to pay more, you either have to put in an excessive amount of unpaid extra work or allow the overrun to prejudice other assignments and limit your marketing activities. Some contracts such as the standard one issued by the Institute of Management Consultants insert a clause to the effect that, although the estimate was prepared in good faith, it *was* only an estimate and is therefore subject to revision should unforeseeable circumstances arise. Such a clause might be helpful, but some clients will still argue that the contract was a fixed price one and that the consultant must live with it.

Preparing estimates

Time estimates should be prepared analytically; that is, the time taken for each activity in each stage of the assignment should be calculated, and the parts added up to produce the total time. For example, in a job evaluation assignment, you would need to prepare job descriptions for each benchmark job. Experience tells you that it takes about a half a day per job (one hour for the interview, one and a half hours to prepare the draft and one hour to clear the draft with the job holder and his or her manager). If you have 20 benchmark jobs, you will take 10 days in all. The other components of the assignment could be estimated on similar lines. A complete estimate for the job would look like this:

Stage	Activity	Time – consultant days
1	Collect basic data	2
2	Prepare, issue and collect questionnaires	1
3	Prepare benchmark job descriptions	10
4	Carry out preliminary ranking exercise for benchmark jobs	1
5	Use analytical scheme to evaluate and grade benchmark jobs	1
6	Supervise preparation of non-benchmark job descriptions	2
7	Slot non-benchmark jobs into grade structure	1
8	Analyse salary survey data	1
9	Prepare salary structure	2
10	Devise salary administration procedures	2
		23

An estimate produced in this form provides a good base for monitoring the progress of the assignment. You should regularly compare actuals with budget so that you can take action as necessary to catch up with lost time.

It is advisable to add 10 per cent or so to your first estimate for contingencies, more if you are on unfamiliar ground. In the above example your estimate could be 25 days. If your fee rate is £500 a day the total estimated cost of the assignment would be £12,500, plus VAT at the standard rate, plus expenses necessarily incurred in the course of the assignment.

Variations to estimates
Analytical estimating along the lines described above is the best technique, but there will always be plenty of scope for variation. One of the factors you may need to take into account is how much clients will do for themselves. In a job evaluation assignment, for example, much of the

work required to prepare job descriptions could be carried out by the client's staff under the consultant's supervision. The time estimate for this activity could then easily be halved.

There is often a range between the minimum time needed to do a basic job and the optimum time required for a Rolls-Royce job. Judgement is required when deciding where to pitch your estimate. And in making pricing judgements you will have to take account of the competition (you are likely to be pitching for the job alongside three or four competitors) and the price sensitivity of your client. It is obviously dangerous to pitch too low, even if you are desperate to get the job. Low bids will only lead you into trouble later on and clients may not be impressed by what they could perceive to be a cheap and nasty approach.

One way to avoid frightening clients too much with the cost of your proposal is to provide an estimate of the fees for the basic job and then add some optional extras. You can indicate in the proposal as strongly as possible the desirability of these extras but explain that a decision on incorporating them would best be made during the course of the assignment when what is needed will become clearer. This approach could impress your client, who would appreciate the fact that the consultant is realistic enough to know that he or she does not know all the answers from the outset and that some may only emerge after deeper analysis has taken place. The danger of this tactic is that the client might gladly accept the basic proposal and reject the extras, in which case you will have sacrificed an opportunity to get more work.

Negotiating

Avoid negotiating fees if you possibly can, but clients will sometimes respond to your proposal with the request that you reduce its cost. You should never contemplate replying with an offer to reduce your fee rates. Neither should you reduce your time estimate. To do so would be to imply that you had overestimated in the first place. The only approach open to you in these circumstances is to reduce the scale of your contribution to the project. This could take the form of cutting out or postponing any parts of the proposal which are not essential to achieving its fundamental objectives. Alternatively, you could suggest that a higher proportion of the work should be carried out by the client's staff under your supervision. Obviously, you should not contemplate either of these tactics if you believe it would prejudice the success of the assignment. Your professional integrity must be given priority, even if it means losing the job. You should never allow yourself to be put into the position of haggling over fees. In any case, clients who haggle are not the sort of clients you want to have. However, there are clients who quite genuinely can only work within a budget which has been imposed upon them, and there will be circumstances when, without sacrificing your professional standards, you can tailor your proposal to their needs.

Increasing profits without increasing fees

There are many ways you can increase your profits apart from raising fees. Naturally, clients are not always going to appreciate your reasons for increasing your fees, so through careful tactics other effective methods could be used to increase your profits. Some methods you may wish to consider are as follows:

- Keep your overall fixed overheads down. Consider the ways of saving costs on space, telephone and personnel.
- Use company cars, space and supplies wherever possible.
- Obtain the client's agreement to supply necessary support services such as secretarial and clerical, mail rooms, postage, delivery service and other support services and personnel. This will keep your administration costs down.
- Obtain approval to charge authorized purchases pertaining to the project to the client.
- Keep an accurate record of all out-of-pocket expenses incurred pertaining to the client's project, document them and invoice for them properly.
- Arrange with the client to pay you in advance for any entertainment or travel expenses you anticipate. That way you can use the client's money and provide an accounting for any extra funds.
- If you are consulting on an hourly basis, attempt to arrange to be at your client's office or project for a full day if possible, rather than a portion of the day.
- Transportation costs and time of travel are not always accurately reflected in the adjustments with the client.
- Determine a minimum fee requirement. The time and costs of a proposal, and the administrative work required by a project, will dictate a minimum fee and profit before you make a proposal.
- Avoid giving away free consulting. There are techniques to avoid giving away your time, which is worth money. This will increase your effective utilisation rate and therefore increase profits. The various ways of avoiding free consulting are covered in Chapter 7.
- Increase your rates for work requested outside regular business hours. A premium fee should be charged for work performed at weekends, during evenings or for part of a day. This suggestion also

applies when clients ask that their project be given priority over other projects.

- Consider obtaining advance payment on account for projected initial or total disbursements if they are considerable. The deposit can be collecting interest for your benefit. As discussed previously, you should consider negotiating in advance for a sizeable deposit if your services are in demand and you are expending time for the client at the expense of other client work you could do.

- Review your credit policy regularly. If you extend credit, make sure your receivables are promptly collected; otherwise you will be paying more interest to the bank on your operating line of credit loan.

- Try to minimise bad debts by adopting the various procedures suggested in Chapter 18, with modifications for your own situation and after your solicitor's advice. Eliminating bad debts is a very effective way of increasing your profits.

- Consider negotiating a bonus with a client for meeting contract needs. For example, if you complete a project for less than the amount allocated in the budget, you could negotiate a percentage of the saving. If your client has deadline schedules, you could agree to give the project priority, which would involve considerable overtime and other disruptions for you, and negotiate a bonus for the number of days you are ahead of the deadline.

Chapter 9
Conducting Consultancy Assignments

Assignment stages

A typical assignment will consist of the following stages:

1. *Background data.* During this stage the consultant obtains
   background data about the client's objectives, plans, operations
   and people in the areas relevant to the assignment. It is particularly
   important to get to know the staff with whom the consultant has
   to interact. This is the time when mutual trust and understanding
   must be established. Managers, staff and trade unions are often
   hostile to management consultants because they are perceived to be
   a threat to their security (the 'hatchet men' syndrome) or because
   they feel that they will be subjected to criticism by an outsider
   who, they believe, cannot understand their problems. Overriding
   these specific fears there is the natural fear of change as something
   which might act against their interests.
2. *Background review.* When the background data has been assembled
   it is useful to pause to analyse it and assess implications. It may be
   necessary in the light of any new facts that have emerged to
   amend the terms of reference and/or the assignment programme.
   This may be the time to call a progress or 'milestone' meeting.
3. *Present arrangements.* In this key stage a detailed review of the
   present arrangements is carried out. The objective is to obtain
   information which will form the basis of the proposed new
   arrangements. An analysis is carried out of strengths and
   weaknesses and areas where improvement or change is required.
   For example, in an organisation assignment the present
   arrangements study would include analysis of activities,
   relationships and the processes of management (delegation,
   decision-making, planning, controlling etc) existing in the
   organisation. Organisation charts and job descriptions would be
   collected or prepared.

4. *Present arrangements review.* The review of present arrangements will highlight strengths, weaknesses, problems and opportunities. It will indicate the lines along which proposals might be developed and implemented. Again, there should be a progress or 'milestone' meeting with the client during which a report can be made of findings to date and possible ways forward can be explored. This is the time to test reactions before pursuing too far a line that may be unproductive or unacceptable. In a large or complex assignment it may be advisable to hold interim progress meetings at regular intervals or at key decision points.

5. *Development of proposals.* In this stage the assembled data and interim findings are examined and proposals are prepared for dealing with the problem of satisfying needs. It is essential to work as closely with the client as possible so that alternative solutions can be assessed and tested jointly. This is the time when you have to win your client's agreement. You should not wait until you issue a final report. You are now going through a process of optimisation. You think you know what should be done, but the client may have different ideas. Your job is to integrate these views with your own so that a solution is produced which is acceptable to all concerned. This should not be a compromise. In fact, a proper discussion of divergences can often produce a solution which is better than either of those originally put forward.

6. *Proposals review.* Ideally there should have been a continuous dialogue between the consultant and the client during the assignment. But when proposals are being developed, it is still desirable to hold one or more formal meetings to discuss the consultant's conclusions. This is when you can finally put your ideas to the test before committing yourself in a formal report. It is much easier for consultants to tackle the practicality of their suggestions at this stage than when they have recorded their views in a formal report. Modifications can be introduced without loss of face and changes can be made in the presentation of the proposals which will enhance their acceptability without destroying their essence. Excellent reports are too often rejected or ignored by clients because of one or two relatively minor points which could easily have been covered earlier. It is during this proposals review that discussions can take place about implementation.

The client may wish to implement without your help, but more often than not it is desirable for the consultant to be involved in implementation, even if this is only on a part-time or occasional basis. In some assignments, of course, implementation is a continuous process as part of the project. For example, a job evaluation engagement might include the design of a job evaluation scheme and an evaluation of jobs by the consultant during the course of the assignment.

7. *Report.* Many assignments conclude with a formal report which contains the consultant's findings, conclusions and recommendations. Except in overseas and some public sector assignments, clients are nowadays reacting against the long, weighty report which was too often allowed to gather dust on shelves without ever being read properly. Clients are expecting much more pithy documents and are sometimes happy to accept a formal presentation at the end of the assignment, backed up by summarised notes and an action plan. In some assignments interim progress reports with a final summary will suffice. However, there often has to be some form in which the outcome of the assignment is summarised and the basic principles of report writing are discussed later in this chapter.

8. *Implementation.* Consultants may work full time on helping the client to implement. More frequently, consultants provide further but diminishing advisory services as the client progressively takes on the full responsibility for operating the new system of whatever has been the outcome of the project.

The consulting process

Problem definition
As the study proceeds the consultant should be working with the problem in such a way that more useful definitions emerge naturally. Since most clients – like people generally – are ambivalent about their need for help with their most important problems, the consultant must skilfully respond to the client's implicit needs.

Analysis
Consultants spend much of their time subjecting complex situations to close and systematic examination and resolving them into their key elements. This process of identification and dissection facilitates the orderly arrangement of a mass of data, which may be present in a confused state, into logical patterns, thus promoting understanding and pointing the way to an appropriate decision.

Analysis concentrates on facts rather than opinions and looks at causes rather than symptoms. It sorts out the problem, clarifying what it is and what it is not. Through analysis, a precise structure and terminology are provided which serve as a means of communication, enabling consultants and their clients to make their diagnoses within a clearly defined framework and in a concrete context.

Diagnosis

Analysis leads to diagnosis: the identification of the likely causes of the problem. Much of management consultants' value lies in their expertise as diagnosticians. It is their job to find out what is actually happening and to define what should happen. The deviation between what is and what should be is the problem to be solved.

Consultants study symptoms but they penetrate behind the surface to identify causes. Causal factors may sometimes be obvious, but are often hidden. And difficulties in identifying causes are particularly acute when the situation has been strongly influenced by the behaviour of the people involved, which is usually the case. Politics, power ploys, conflict, demotivated executives or staff, poor quality people, inadequate team work can all contribute to the creation of a problem.

As Arthur Turner wrote in the *Harvard Business Review* (September-October 1982):

> Competent diagnosis requires more than an examination of the external environment, the technology and economics of the business, and the behaviour of non-managerial members of the organisation. The consultant must also ask why executives made certain choices that now appear to be mistakes or ignored certain factors that now seem important.

Although the need for independent diagnosis is often cited as a reason for using outsiders, drawing members of the client organisation into the diagnostic process makes good sense. Hypotheses can be tested and the practicalities of alternative courses of action assessed. A consultant quoted by Arthur Turner explained:

> We usually insist that client team members are assigned to the project. They, not us, must do the detail work. We'll help, we'll push – but they'll do it. While this is going on, we talk with the CEO every day for an hour or two about the issues that are surfacing, and we meet with the chairman once a week. In this way we diagnose strategic problems in connection with organisational issues. We get some sense of the skills of the key people – what they can do and how they work. When we emerge with strategic and organisational recommendations, they are usually well accepted because they have been thoroughly tested.

84

Problem-solving

The processes of analysis and diagnosis lead naturally into the problem-solving stage in which alternative solutions are listed and evaluated against the objectives set for the exercise. Essentially, the evaluation is an attempt to decide whether or not a particular course of action will correct the deviation and point the organisation in the appropriate direction.

But in this process of weighing up possible courses of action, do not expect the system to produce a black-and-white solution. Remember what Drucker wrote:

> A decision is a judgement. It is a choice between alternatives. It is rarely a choice between right and wrong. It is at best a choice between almost right and probably wrong – but much more often a choice between two courses of action, neither of which is probably more right than the other.

The trouble with many assignments is that clients expect consultants to come up with one right solution. Equally, consultants feel bound to produce clearly and unequivocally the perfect answer. This often leads to theoretically good solutions which won't work, or at least which the client feels won't work. The only answer to this difficulty is to get clients involved so that they understand that there are valid alternatives and can, after joint evaluation, agree on balance an optimum solution with which they will feel comfortable.

Recommending actions

Consultants spend a great deal of time writing reports in which the information and analysis are clearly presented and the recommendations are convincingly related to the diagnosis upon which they are based. Many consultants feel that their job has been done when they present a consistent and logical action plan of steps designed to improve the diagnosed situation. They recommend and the client decides whether and how to implement.

As Arthur Turner wrote:

> This set up is simplistic and unsatisfactory. Untold numbers of seemingly convincing reports, submitted at great expense, have no real impact because – due to the constraints outside the consultant's assumed bailiwick – the relationship stops at the formulation of theoretically sound recommendations that can't be implemented.

To avoid this problem you must continually test your proposals with the clients to sound out their reactions. In a successful assignment the consultant continually strives to understand what actions, if recommended, are likely to be implemented and where people are prepared to do things differently. Recommendations may have to be confined to those steps the consultant believes will be implemented well.

This raises the perennial question of whether consultants should recommend what they know is right or what they know will be accepted. The purists will say that a consultant is bound as a professional adviser to recommend the 'best' solution. Realists will argue that the 'best' solution will be one that the client will accept and that there is little point in recommending actions that will not be taken. What is theoretically best, as consultants see it (and how certain can they be that they are right?), is not necessarily best in practice. To take an arrogant and rigid professional view is not likely to get a consultant far.

The art of persuasion

On the other hand, consultants are not paid just to tell clients what they want to hear. Consultants are there to convince clients that a particular course of action is likely to be beneficial, practical and cost-effective. The art of persuasion is an important one for consultants to develop, and there are six simple rules that you must follow. These were defined by Michael Armstrong in *How To Be An Even Better Manager* (Kogan Page, 1988) as follows:

Six rules for effective persuasion
1. *Define your objective and get the facts.* Decide what you want to achieve and why. Assemble all the facts you need to support your case. Eliminate emotional arguments so that you and others can judge the proposition on the facts alone.
2. *Find out what the client wants.* Never underestimate a person's natural resistance to change. But bear in mind that such resistance is proportional, not to the extent of the change, but to the extent to which it affects the individual personally. When asked to accept a proposition, the first questions even a rational person asks are: 'How does this affect me?', 'What do I stand to lose?', 'What do I stand to gain?'. These questions must be answered before persuasion can start.

   The key to all persuasion is to see your proposition from the other person's point of view. You must find out how clients look at things – what they want. Listen to what they have to say. Don't talk too much. Ask questions to explore understanding.
3. *Prepare a simple and attractive presentation.* Your presentation should

be as simple and straightforward as possible. Highlight the benefits. Don't bury the selling points. Lead gently so that there are no surprises. Anticipate objections.

4. *Make the client a party to your ideas.* Get clients to contribute. Find some common ground to start off with agreement. Don't antagonise them. Avoid defeating them in arguments. Help them to preserve their self-esteem. Always leave them a way out.

5. *Positively sell the benefits.* Show conviction. You will fail to persuade if you don't believe in what you are saying and don't communicate that belief. Spell out the benefits. What you are proposing may be of less interest to the individuals concerned than the effects of that proposal on them.

6. *Clinch and take action.* Make sure that you do not push too hard (over-persuasive tactics can be counter-productive – agreement should come naturally). But when you reach your objective don't stay and risk losing it. Take prompt follow-up action. There is no point in going to all the trouble of getting agreement if you let things slide afterwards.

Change management

Consultants are catalysts. They act as change agents. But to carry out this role they have to understand how to manage change.

It is always said that people automatically resist change. This is not so. There are many people who strive for change and welcome it – the desire for new experience underlies much of human behaviour. But they have to feel that this new experience is worth having, that they will benefit from it in some way. They have to 'own' the solution to the problem. Michael Armstrong has suggested ten ways of minimising resistance to change:

Ten ways of minimising resistance to change
Resistance to change will be less if:

1. participants have jointly diagnosed the problem;
2. the change has been agreed by group decisions;
3. those affected by change feel that they can accept the project as their own, not one imposed upon them by outsiders, ie consultants;
4. the change has the wholehearted support of management;
5. the change fits the culture of the organisation and accords with well-established values;
6. the change is seen as reducing rather than increasing present burdens;

7. the change offers the kind of new experience which interests participants;
8. participants feel that their autonomy and security are not threatened;
9. those advocating change understand the feelings and fears of those affected and take steps to relieve unnecessary fears;
10. it is recognised that new ideas are likely to be misinterpreted and ample provision is made for discussion of reactions to proposals.

Resistance to change is often more acute if it comes as a shock to the system. The consultant should avoid surprises. This is why saving everything up for a final block-busting report is often a mistake. It follows that consultants should persuade their clients to experiment with new procedures during the course of an engagement, and not wait until the end of the project before beginning to implement change. When innovations prove successful they are institutionalised more effectively than when simply recommended without some demonstration of their value.

Process consulting

Much of what was said above about the consultancy process can be summed up in the expression 'process consulting'. This is a way of describing an approach to consultancy which is most likely to lead to success in any situation where the assignment is about implementing change rather than simply providing information. And change is the objective of nearly all consultancy engagements.

As described by Ed Schein, process consultants seek to give their clients 'insight' into what is going on around them and between them and other people. The events to be observed, and learned from, are primarily the various human actions which occur in the normal flow of work, in the conduct of meetings and in formal and informal encounters between members of the organisation. Process consultants also help to define the organisation's culture so that steps can be taken by their clients to preserve what is good about the culture and to modify what is not so good.

Assumptions underlying process consultation

The assumptions underlying process consultation as defined by Ed Schein are:

1. Managers often do not know what is wrong and need special help in diagnosing what their problems actually are.
2. Managers often do not know what kinds of help consultants can

give to them; they need to be helped to know what kind of help to seek.

3. Most managers have a constructive intent to improve things but need help in identifying what to improve and how to improve it.
4. Most organisations can be more effective if they learn to diagnose their own strengths and weaknesses. No organisational form is perfect; hence every form of organisation will have some weaknesses for which compensatory mechanisms need to be found.
5. A consultant could probably not, without exhaustive and time-consuming study, learn enough about the culture of the organisation to suggest reliable new courses of action. Therefore, he must work jointly with members of the organisation who *do* know the culture intimately from having lived within it.
6. The client must learn to see the problem for himself, to share in the diagnosis, and to be actively involved in generating a remedy. One of the process consultant's roles is to provide new and challenging alternatives for the client to consider. Decision-making about these alternatives must, however, remain in the hands of the client.
7. It is of prime importance that the process consultant be expert in how to *diagnose* and how to *establish effective helping relationships* with clients. Effective process consultation involves the passing on of both these skills.

Managing the assignment

An assignment is a project and project management techniques should therefore be applied. The activities required are:

1. *Terms of reference.* Ensure that these are clear and fully understood by everyone concerned.
2. *Outcomes.* The outcome of the assignment should be defined, ie how the terms of reference will be met and in what form (eg, report, presentation, progressive implementation).
3. *Performance criteria.* The criteria upon which the success of the project will be based should be agreed.
4. *Programme.* Programming the project requires:

   (a) a list of the major activities in sequence;
   (b) a breakdown of each major activity into subsidiary tasks;
   (c) an analysis of the interrelationships and interdependencies of major and subsidiary tasks;
   (d) an estimate of the time required to complete each activity and task;

(e) a resource plan for making available the consultancy skills required at each stage of the assignment;

(f) a time budget for the assignment which, in accordance with the proposal, budgets time on a weekly basis for each activity and task. Separate budgets should be prepared for each consultant on the assignment. The budget can be expressed for the assignment as a whole on the assignment control sheet (Chapter 17, Figure 17.10) and for individual consultants on the consultant's brief and budget sheet (Chapter 17, Figure 17.1);

(g) a cash flow forecast, estimating the in-flow of fees and the out-flow of expenses.

the programme could be expressed in a bar chart as in the example given in Figure 9.1.

In more complex assignments a network could be drawn up. Network analysis or critical path planning represents the component parts of the project as a network of interrelated activities and highlights those activities which are critical to the progress and completion of the project and upon which later or interrelated activities depend (see Bibliography (page 228) for references to books on network planning).

6. *Consultants' brief.* Any additional consultants or subcontractors working on the assignment should be briefed on what they are required to do, and how and by when they are expected to do it. Such briefing should preferably be in writing.

5. *'Milestone' or progress meetings.* The timing, purpose and membership of 'milestone' or progress meetings should be determined.

7. *Monitoring.* Arrangements should be made to monitor the progress of the assignment against the terms of reference, the programme and the time budget. It is advisable for the consultant to keep a diary of events during each week which details the time spent on the assignment each day and any expenses incurred. The diary should compare progress with plan and should highlight problems and variances. If there is any slippage, the reasons must be investigated and recorded. If remedial action is not possible, the client must be informed and an amended programme agreed.

If any extra work is required that was not included in the original proposal and terms of reference, it is essential to have the client's agreement in writing to the additional costs that will be incurred and to any changes in the timetable. Assignments can end

Ref. no.	Description	Consultant days	1	2	3	4	5	6	7	8	9	10
									Weeks			
1	Collect basic data	2	---									
2	Prepare, issue and collect questionnaires	1		---	---							
3	Prepare benchmark job descriptions	10				---	---					
4	Carry out preliminary ranking exercise for benchmark jobs	1						---				
5	Evaluate benchmark jobs	1						---				
6	Supervise preparation of non-benchmark job descriptions	2							---	---		
7	Slot non-benchmark jobs into grade structure	1									---	
8	Analyse salary survey data	1									---	
9	Prepare salary structure	2										---
10	Devise salary admin procedures	2										---

- - - = non-continuous   ——— = continuous

Figure 9.1. *Assignment programme*

on a sour note if fees are above the estimate for a reason which has not been previously explained to and agreed by the client.

The types of records that can be used to control assignments are described in Chapter 17.

Report writing

Although a lengthy completion report is not always a feature of the end of an assignment, consultants are usually very much in the business of report writing. The report is a visible record of what has been accomplished and the success of an assignment will often be measured – fairly or unfairly – by the quality of the report.

A typical report will contain:

(a) an introduction setting out objectives (terms of reference) and describing the approach adopted;
(b) a summary of conclusions and recommendations;
(c) a description of present arrangements;
(d) an analysis of the strengths and weaknesses of the present arrangements;
(e) proposals on what needs to be done to enhance strengths and remove weaknesses;
(f) a statement of the costs and benefits of implementing proposals;
(g) an implementation plan and programme;
(h) appendices which contain supporting statistical data and other detailed information which is best kept out of the body of the report.

The Bibliography (page 228) contains references to texts on report writing. The following is a list of the main points to consider when preparing and writing a report.

Structure
1. The report should have a logical structure consisting of:
    (a) an introduction which states:
        – the report's aims, terms of reference and why it should be read
        – the sources of information on which the report is based
        – the arrangement of the report;
    (b) a central part which contains:
        – the assembled facts and the analysis of the facts
        – the diagnosis

- the logic leading from the analysis, to the diagnosis, to the conclusions on what action needs to be taken
- a review of alternative courses of action (if appropriate) setting out the pros and cons of each but indicating clearly the most favoured action;

(c) a final section which sets out:
- recommendations, with a statement of how they will help to achieve the stated aims of the report or overcome any weaknesses revealed by the analytical study
- the benefits and costs of implementing the recommendations
- the suggested method of proceeding, the actions that have to be taken, the programme of work required, the time scales involved and the resources needed.

Language
2. Meaning should be conveyed without ambiguity and without giving unnecessary trouble to the reader by:
   (a) using no more words than are necessary to express your meaning, avoiding the use of superfluous adjectives and adverbs;
   (b) using familiar words rather than jargon;
   (c) using words with a precise meaning rather than those that are vague;
   (d) using active verbs wherever possible to make comments and recommendations more lively and compelling;
   (e) keeping sentences short and to the point.

Presentation
3. The way in which you present your report affects its impact and value. The reader should be able to follow your arguments easily and not be sidetracked or bogged down in too much detail.
4. Paragraphs should be short and restricted to a single topic. If you want to list or highlight a series of points, tabulate them.
5. Paragraphs should be numbered for ease of reference.
6. Use headings to guide people on what they are about to read and to help them find their way about the report.
7. Do not clutter up the main pages of your report with masses of indigestible figures or other data. Summarise key statistics in compact, easy-to-follow tables with clear headings. Use graphs sparingly to illustrate a point or trend. Relegate supporting material to appendices.

Presentations

Consultants often have to address client meetings during an assignment to present their interim findings or their final recommendations. The Bibliography (page 228) includes references to books on public speaking, but the following list covers the main points you should consider when preparing and delivering presentations.

Preparation

1. Start by defining your objective. Then decide the main messages you want to get across.
2. List the main messages and the points you want to make against each message.
3. Collect the data you want to support your message.
4. Structure your presentation, arranging the points in a logical order, leading from your introduction to a positive conclusion. The analysis should lead inexorably to the diagnosis which should lead inevitably to the recommendation.
5. Prepare your notes – one card for each heading with a summary of the points you want to make.
6. Prepare visual aids to illustrate and underline your message.
7. Rehearse to achieve confidence and fluency and to get your timing right (you should not speak for more than 45 minutes).
8. Check arrangements for visual aids on site.

Delivery

9. Ensure that you are audible.
10. Vary pace, pitch and emphasis.
11. Highlight key points by emphasis and with visual aids.
12. Try to be conversational. Avoid a stilted delivery. If you *must* read your presentation, practise it sufficiently well to ensure that you speak naturally, without burying your head in your script.
13. Use simple, short words and sentences.
14. Keep your eyes on the audience.
15. Use hands for gesture and emphasis only. Avoid fidgeting. Don't put your hands in your pockets (if you have any pockets).
16. Stand naturally and upright, not casually. Look like someone in command. Don't pace up and down.

Chapter 10

Practice Development

There are many ways of acquiring clients and developing your practice. The simplest way is to keep your existing clients happy and nurture the present and past clients well. Studies show that over 70 per cent of a consultant's business is based on repeat business or referral business from existing clients. A marketing formula shows that the average person has over 200 contacts including friends, relatives and associates. By carefully developing this client potential you can expand your practice rapidly.

For example, from one satisfied client you could obtain enough projects sufficient to keep you busy on an ongoing basis. If your client gives you repeat work regularly and also recommends you to 10 other business associates in the same industry and five of them become clients, your business will grow. Former employees of the first client or referral clients may go to work for other firms in the private or public sector. If they enjoyed working with you, they will request your services again or refer work to you. The possibilities are limitless.

An effective way of keeping your clients satisfied is to create client dependency. The more the client relies on you because of your speciality, the more repeat business you will generate. The more your client respects you for your knowledge and leadership, the more the client will look to you for guidance.

It is important that the client feels in control at all times. You must maintain your image as a unique commodity. Your role is to complement staff. You do not want to be perceived as just another person on the staff.

If there are particular tasks that the client does not enjoy, and you can fill the void and have the skills and ability to perform the task, and the situation seems appropriate, this could create further dependency. If the outcome of a project is particularly successful and considerable positive feedback occurs, make a point of having your client share the glory with you. A satisfied client will appreciate your value, and provide you with more consulting contracts.

There are other ways of developing your practice. Expanding your line by adding additional services that are natural extensions of your first service is effective. If you have clients who retain you for one service, you are creating a potential two- or three-fold growth pattern with all your clientele. Because you already have the credibility with the client for one project, it will be much easier for you to market your skills for the other services.

Subcontracting is another way of expanding your practice. You can locate subcontractors from your contract contact network and through referral. They can be effectively used to increase your earnings by providing depth and greater capacity for your business. You would be in a position to make proposals for larger or more complex projects using past, present or future clients as your base. If a client has been satisfied with your service on a smaller project or a particular service line, and you have additional service lines and a greater depth and capacity, the prospects are endless. Naturally, subcontracting will involve more administration for you, but the independent contractor status of subconsultants will allow you flexibility to hire them as necessary.

Other ways of expanding your practice are to review continually all aspects of your operation, note the weak areas and develop a specific plan for dealing with them. Areas such as self-promotion and more efficient follow-up on leads can also enhance your clientele base.

Market development plan

Your practice development programme should be expressed as a market development plan. This does three basic things:

1. It sums up the present situation.
2. It defines where you want to go.
3. It describes how you intend to get there.

Your marketing plan should be structured as follows:

1. Analysis of present situation

- A description of what type of consultancy business you are in;
- A review of achievements over the last 12 months or since the last marketing plan was prepared – fee income, profit, utilisation rate (chargeable time) and new clients;
- An assessment of the strengths of your consultancy:
  - what have you got to offer?
  - what have been your successes, and why?
- An assessment of the weaknesses of your consultancy:

- what can you not offer that you should be able to?
- what have been your failures and why did they happen?
- are your resources adequate in terms of skills and finance?
● A review of the opportunities available to you as indicated by an assessment of the market:
    - does your analysis of the services offered by other consultants suggest a gap that you could fill, ie is there any niche in the market that you can and should move into?
    - are there additional services which you believe you can and should offer?
● An assessment of the threats facing your consultancy:
    - is the demand for your services slackening?
    - are you losing market-share to other consultants?
    - are you losing too many jobs to competitors?

2. Targets

● Utilisation rate
● Fee income
● Profit
● Market-share
● Success rate in obtaining assignments
● New clients
● New sectors
● New services
● Publicity

3. Action plan for practice development

● Marketing campaign – extending network, direct mail, new brochure, advertising, follow-up with clients etc;
● Publicity campaign – articles, lectures, mentions in the press etc;
● Product development – developing new services and improving existing services;
● Skill development – improving skills in selling, conducting assignments, presentations, report writing etc;
● Profit enhancement – taking steps to improve the profitability of assignments;
● Overhead cost control – paring down excessive overheads and unnecessary expenses;
● Tax planning – making the best use of the scope for tax avoidance.

Part 2

Chapter 11

Setting Up Your Consultancy Business

The three ingredients for success

The three ingredients for running a successful consultancy business are to:

(a) possess the necessary consultancy skills and attributes;
(b) obtain high utilisation of chargeable time by effective marketing and selling;
(c) achieve maximum profitability by running the consultancy in a business-like way.

The first two ingredients were covered in Part 1. The third was partly dealt with in Part 1, especially in Chapter 8 on fees and estimates, but the wider aspects of setting up and operating the consultancy business will be described in this part.

Set-up checklist

The following is a checklist of the points you should consider when setting up your consultancy:

1. Assess your own capabilities and potential as a consultant (Chapter 3).
2. Decide what sort of consultancy business you want to be in (Chapters 2 and 4).
3. Assess the potential market for your services (Chapter 4).
4. Decide on your fee structure (Chapter 8).
5. Prepare an initial marketing plan (Chapter 10).
6. Calculate start-up costs (Chapter 11).
7. Prepare a business plan (Chapter 12).
8. Select your business and professional advisers (Chapter 13).
9. Decide on the structure of your business (Chapter 14).
10. Decide on the name of your business (Chapter 14).
11. Raise finance (Chapter 15).

12. Set up your office (Chapter 16).
13. Set up record systems (Chapter 17).
14. Set up credit, invoicing and collection procedures (Chapter 18).
15. Prepare a tax plan (Chapter 19).
16. Prepare standard contracts (Chapter 20).
17. Take out general insurances (Chapter 21).
18. Set up a pension plan (Chapter 21).
19. Decide how to deal with professional liability (Chapter 22).

Start-up costs and monthly expenses

It is necessary to estimate your start-up costs and monthly business and personal expenses before taking any further steps to set up the consultancy. Remember that if you are starting from scratch your fee income may be low in the initial months. You may not even generate enough fees to cover your start-up costs and expenses in the first year of operation, when you will be busy marketing and slowly but steadily building up your reputation. You therefore need these preliminary estimates not only for planning purposes but also to indicate how much finance you might need to raise (see Chapter 15 for a discussion of methods of raising finance).

Start-up costs
Start-up costs will depend largely on your circumstances – the amount of equipment you already have, the amount you feel you need and the projected scale of your marketing and consultancy operations. If you work on your own from home all you may need is an inexpensive word processor, a telephone answering machine, stationery, basic office supplies and some advice from an accountant or the Small Firms Service. You could get away with less than £2000 if you were careful. But a sole practitioner could easily spend £10,000 or more if he or she purchased a full range of equipment, obtained a considerable quantity of professional advice and launched an expensive marketing and public relations campaign.

The following checklist sets out the main headings you should consider when estimating start-up costs.

Start-up cost checklist

Equipment and supplies (other than stationery)
1. Computer/word processor
2. Typewriter
3. Duplicator

4. Fax machine
5. Telex machine
6. Office furniture
7. Telephone answering machine
8. Dictating machine/tape recorder
9. Calculator
10. Other office equipment and supplies such as binders, staplers, punches, paper clips etc

Stationery and printing
11. Headed paper
12. Visiting cards
13. Headed report folders
14. Brochure
15. Files and folders
16. Diaries
17. Other paper requirements

Professional services (initial advice)
18. Accountancy
19. Legal
20. Financial
21. Design consultancy
22. PR consultancy

Marketing and PR
23. Direct mail campaign
24. Advertising
25. Travel costs
26. Entertaining
27. Consultant register fees
28. Other marketing or PR expenditure

Miscellaneous expenses
29. Licence if practising as an employment agency or a financial adviser
30. Professional subscriptions
31. Rent deposit on office
32. Other

Monthly expenses

Checklist of business operating expenses (not claimable from clients)

Office (space and services)
1. Rent and rates
2. Heating and lighting
3. Telephone
4. Service charge

Office operational costs
5. Lease or hire of equipment
6. Stationery and office supplies
7. Other printing costs
8. Answer service
9. Postal charges

Services
10. Word processing and typing (agency costs)
11. Accountant
12. Solicitor

Car(s)
13. Lease or contract hire costs
14. Hire purchase repayments
15. Depreciation
16. Running costs: fuel, repairs, maintenance, AA/RAC subscriptions
17. Insurance
18. Road fund licence

Travel
19. Rail
20. Air

Insurance
21. Office
22. Jury service
23. Business travel
24. Employer's liability
25. Professional liability

Interest
26. On mortgage
27. On bank or other loans

Marketing
28. Direct mailing
29. Advertising
30. Entertaining
31. Public relations

Professional
32. Professional subscriptions
33. Conferences
34. Training courses
35. Journals and magazines
36. Books

Personnel
37. Salaries
38. National Insurance
39. Pension
40. Sick or maternity leave costs (additional costs of employing temporary replacements)
41. Life and medical insurance

Miscellaneous
42. Licence fees, where applicable
43. Other

Monthly personal expenses checklist (pro-rated where appropriate)
1. Housing – mortgage payments or rent, rates, insurance
2. Food and drink
3. Clothing
4. Car – hire purchase, lease or contract hire, repairs, maintenance, fuel, insurance
5. Heating, lighting, telephone
6. Life and medical insurance
7. Personal pension
8. Loan repayments
9. Credit card charges
10. Travel
11. Recreation
12. Education (family)
13. Medical and dental
14. Donations
15. Savings
16. Other

Advice on setting up your business

Before going any further you should seek preliminary advice from your accountant, your solicitor and your bank manager, and guidance on selecting these professional advisers is given in Chapter 13. You can also get advice from your regional Small Firms Centre. This will provide consultancy services and a wide range of useful publications. Information is free and counselling incurs only a modest charge.

Chapter 12

Preparing Your Business Plan

Why prepare a plan?

Most consultants prefer to be a consultant first and a business owner second, but planning and good management skills are vital to business success. Those who do not plan run a very high risk of failure. If you do not know where you are going in your personal or business life, there is little prospect that you will arrive. A business plan is a written summary of what you hope to accomplish by being in business, and how you intend to organise your resources to meet your goals. It is an essential guide for operating your business successfully and measuring progress along the way.

Planning forces you to think ahead and visualise; it encourages realistic thinking instead of over-optimism. It helps you to identify your clients, your market area, your pricing strategy and the competitive conditions under which you must operate. This process often leads to the discovery of new opportunities as well as deficiencies in your plan.

Having clear goals and a well-written plan assists decision-making. You can always change your goals, but at least with a business plan you have some basis and a standard comparison to use in evaluating alternatives presented to you.

A business plan establishes the amount of financing or outside investment required and when it is needed. It makes it much easier for a lender or investor to assess your financing proposal and to assess you as a business manager. It inspires confidence in lenders and self-confidence in yourself to know every aspect of the business when you are negotiating your financing. If you have a realistic, comprehensive and well-documented plan, it will assist you greatly in convincing a lender.

Having well-established objectives helps you to analyse your progress. If you have not attained your objectives by a certain period, you will be aware of that fact and can make appropriate adjustments at an early stage.

Three or four hours spent each month updating your plan will save considerable time and money in the long run, and may even save your business. It is essential to develop a habit of planning and constantly reassessing as an integral part of your management style.

Format

The business plan format shown in Figure 12.1 is a starting point for organising your own plan. The comments following the sub-headings should help you to decide which sections are relevant to your business situation.

The business plan format normally consists of four parts: the introduction, the business concept, the financial plan and the appendix.

The plan starts with an introductory page highlighting the business plan. Even though your entire business is described later, a crisp one- or two-page introduction helps to capture the immediate attention of the potential investor or lender.

The business concept is based upon the marketing plan (see Chapter 10). It identifies your market potential and outlines your action plan for the coming year. Make sure your stated business goals are compatible with your personal and financial goals, your management ability and family considerations. The heart of the business concept is your sales forecast for the coming year. As your statement of confidence in your marketing strategy, it forms the basis for your cash flow forecast and projected income statement. This section also contains an assessment of business risks and a contingency plan. Being honest about your business risks and how you plan to deal with them is evidence of sound management.

The financial plan outlines the level of present financing and identifies the financing sought. This section should be brief. The financial plan contains financial forecasts which are projections into the future based on current information and assumptions. In carrying out your action plan for the coming year, these operating forecasts are an essential guide to business survival and profitability. It is important to refer to them often and, if circumstances dictate, recalculate them.

The appendix section contains all the items that do not naturally fall elsewhere in the document, or which expand further on the summaries in the document.

Figure 12.1 *Business plan format*

1. Introductory page
   (a) company name
       - include address and telephone number
   (b) contact person
       - consultant's name and telephone number
   (c) paragraph about company
       - nature of business and market area
   (d) securities offered to investors or lenders
   (e) business loans sought
   (f) summary of proposed use of funds
2. Summary of highlights of business plan
   - preferably one-page maximum
   - include your project, competitive advantage and 'bottom line' needs
3. Table of contents – section titles and page numbers should be given for easy reference
4. Description of the consultancy
   (a) outlook and growth potential
       - outline trends – past, present and future – and new developments
       - state your sources of information
   (b) markets and customers
       - estimated size of total market, share and sales, new requirements and market trends
   (c) competitive companies
       - market share, strengths and weaknesses, profitability, trends
   (d) national and economic trends
       - population shifts, consumer trends, relevant economic indicators
5. Description of business venture
   (a) nature of consulting service
       - characteristics, method of operation, whether performed locally, regionally, nationally or internationally
   (b) target market
       - typical clients identified by groups, present consulting patterns and average earnings, wants and needs
   (c) competitive advantage of your business concept
       - your market niche, uniqueness, estimated market share
   (d) business location and size
       - location relative to market, size of premises, home or office use

    (e) staff and equipment needed
- overall requirement, capacity, home or office use, part- or full-time staff or as required

    (f) brief history
- principals involved in the consulting business or proposed consulting business, development work done, CVs and background experience of principals, CVs of key consulting associates if applicable.

6. Business goals

    (a) one year
- specific goals, such as utilisation rates, fee income, profit margin, share of market, opening new office, introducing new service, etc

    (b) over the longer term
- return on investment, business net worth, sale of business

7. Marketing plan

    (a) sales strategy
- sales objectives, sales tools, sales support
- target clients

    (b) sales approach
- style of operation and techniques

    (c) pricing
- fee structures, costings, break-even analysis

    (d) promotion
- direct mailing, advertising, publicity appropriate to reach target market
- techniques of developing exposure, credibility and contacts

    (e) service policies
- policies that your consulting practice will adopt with regard to credit and collection, bidding, nature of clientele, etc

    (f) guarantees
- service performance guarantees or other assurances will vary depending upon nature of consulting practice and type of contract or client

    (g) tracking methods
- method for confirming who your clients are and how they heard about you.

8. Sales forecast

    (a) assumptions
- one never has all the necessary information, so state all the assumptions made in developing the forecast

    (b) monthly forecast for coming year
- sales volume, projected in £

    (c) annual forecast for following two to four years
        – sales volume, projected in £

The sales forecast is the starting point for your projected income statement and cash flow forecast.

9. Costing plan
    (a) cost of facilities, equipment and materials (as applicable)
        – estimates and quotations
    (b) capital estimates
        – one time start-up or expansion capital required

10. Operations
    (a) purchasing plans
    (b) space required
        – floor and office space, improvements required, expansion capability
    (c) staff and equipment required
        – personnel by skill level
        – fixtures, office equipment
    (d) operations strategy

11. Corporate structure
    (a) legal form
        – sole trader, partnership or incorporation
    (b) share distribution
        – list of principal shareholders
    (c) contracts and agreements
        – list of contracts and agreements in force
        – management contract, shareholder or partnership agreement, service contract, leases
    (d) directors and officers
        – names and addresses, role in company
    (e) background of key management personnel
        – brief CVs of active owners and key employees
    (f) organisation chart
        – identify reporting relationships
    (g) duties and responsibilities of key personnel
        – brief job descriptions – who is responsible for what

12. Supporting professional assistance
    – professionals on contract in specialised or deficient areas; would include solicitor, accountant, banker, insurance broker etc

13. Research and development programme
    – product or service improvements, process improvements, costs and risks

14. Risk assessment
    (a) competitors' reaction

- will competitor try to squeeze you out? What form do
  you anticipate any reaction will take?
  (b) list of critical external factors that might occur
  - identify effects of strikes, recession, new technology, new
    competition, supplier problems, shifts in consumer
    demand, costs of delays and overruns, unfavourable
    industry trends
  (c) list of critical internal factors that might occur
  - income projections not realised, client dispute or
    litigation, receivables difficulties, demand for services
    increases very quickly, key employee or consultant quits
  (d) dealing with risks
  - contingency plan to handle the most significant risks

15. Overall schedule
    - interrelationship and timing of all major events important to
      starting and developing your business

16. Action plan
    (a) steps to accomplish this year's goals
    - flow chart by month or by quarter of specific action to be
      taken and by whom
    (b) checkpoint for measuring results
    - identify significant dates, sales levels as decision points

17. Financial forecast
    If a business has been in operation for a period of time, the
    previous years' balance sheets and income statements are required,
    preferably for the past two or three years.
    (a) opening balance sheet
    - The balance sheet is a position statement, not an historical
      record; it shows what is owned and owed at a given date.
    - Your balance sheet will indicate how your investment has
      grown over a period of time. Investors and lenders
      typically examine balance sheets to see if the company is
      within acceptable assets to liability limits. An example of a
      balance sheet is given in Chapter 17 (Figure 17.7).
    (b) profit and loss forecast (budget)
    - The profit and loss forecast (budget) can be described as the
      operating statement you would expect to see for your
      business at the end of the period for which the forecast is
      being prepared.
    - For a new business, the budget would show what revenue
      and expenses you expect the business to have in its first
      year of operation.
    - It is very useful, of course, to prepare a forecast for a
      period longer than one year. It is suggested that a detailed
      operating budget be prepared for the next year of operation

and a less detailed forecast for the following two years.
- Preparing an income and expense budget for a new business is more difficult than preparing one for an existing business, simply because in a new business there is no historical record to go by. For this reason the preparation of this forecast is an even more essential, interesting and rewarding experience than doing it for an existing business, despite the time and effort required. The question as to whether a profit will be made will be answered by this analysis exercise.
- The fee income statement is the most difficult because it is the most uncertain at the commencement of business. It is essential that a figure be projected on a conservative estimate.
- The main concern is to account for expenses accurately and in as much detail as possible. This will then provide a target or break-even figure towards which to work.
- Some headings may not be appropriate for your type of consulting practice; other headings should be added.
- an example of a profit and loss account is given in Chapter 17 (Figure 17.3). For business planning purposes the best format is the annual budget statement in Chapter 17 (Figure 17.6).
(c) cash flow forecast
- A cash flow budget measures the flow of money in and out of the business. It is critical to you and your banker.
- Many businesses operate on a seasonal basis, as there are slow months and busy months. The cash flow budget projection will provide an indication of the times of a cash flow shortage to assist in planning and financing your operation properly. It will tell you in advance if you have enough cash to get by.
- A cash flow budget should be prepared a year in advance and contain monthly breakdowns.
- see Chapter 17 (Figure 17.5).
(d) cash flow assumptions
When reviewing the cash flow plan, certain assumptions should be made:
- Sales: monthly sales (consulting service fees) that are expected to materialise
- Receipts: cash sales represent cash actually received
- Disbursements: accounts payable to be paid in month following month of purchase
- Accounting and legal: to be paid upon receipt of bill, expected to be after your fiscal year-end financial statements have been completed

- Advertising: anticipated to be the same amount each month and paid for in the month the expense is incurred
- Car expenses: lease, hire purchase, insurance, tax and running expenses, paid for in the month the expense is incurred
- Bank charges and interest: anticipated to be the same amount each month and paid for monthly in same month the expense is incurred
- Equipment rental: to be paid for in monthly payments
- Income taxes: amount for taxes of the previous year and to be paid in the current year
- Insurance: annual premium to be paid quarterly, half-yearly or annually in instalments of equal amounts
- Loan repayment: amount is the same each month and paid in accordance with the monthly schedule furnished by the lending institution
- Office supplies and expenses: to be paid in month following receipt of invoice and supplies to be purchased on a quarterly basis
- Taxes and licences: to be paid for upon receipt of invoice in July
- Telephone: to be paid for quarterly
- Utilities: expected to fluctuate seasonally and to be paid quarterly
- Salaries and benefits: amount considered to be the same each month and paid for in the month the expense is incurred
- Miscellaneous: expected to be the same each month and paid for in the same month the expense is incurred
- Bad debts: varies

(e) Break-even analysis
- The break-even analysis is a critical calculation for every consulting business. Rather than calculating how much your firm would make if it attained an estimated sales volume, a more meaningful analysis determines at what sales volume your firm will break even. An estimated sales volume could be very unreliable as there are many factors which could affect revenue.
- The calculation of a break-even point for every small business is one of the most crucial pieces of information. Above the break-even sales volume it is only a matter of how much money your business can generate; below the break-even level of sales, it is only a matter of how many days a business can operate before bankruptcy.
- A break-even analysis provides a very real and meaningful

figure to work towards and might be required to be updated every few months to reflect your business growth.
- The break-even point is where total costs are equal to total revenues.
- The calculation of total costs is made by adding variable costs on to the fixed costs.
- Total costs are all costs of operating the business over a specified time period.
- Variable costs are those that vary directly with the number of consulting services provided or marketing and promotion activities undertaken. These typically include car expenses, business travel expenses, supplies, brochures, etc when these cannot be passed on to the client.
- Fixed costs are costs that do not generally vary with the number of clients serviced. Also known as indirect costs, these costs typically include salaries, rent, secretarial service, insurance, telephone accounting and legal supplies.
- An example of a break-even analysis was given in Chapter 8, Figure 8.1.

18. Financing and capitalisation
    (a) loan applied for
        - the amount, terms and when required
    (b) purpose of loan
        - attach a detailed description of the aspects of the business to be financed
    (c) owner's equity
        - the amount of your financial commitment to the business
    (d) summary of loan requirements
        - for a particular consulting project or for the business as a whole

19. Operating loan
    (a) overdraft limit applied for
        - a new overdraft or an increase, and security offered
    (b) maximum operating cash required
        - amount required, timing of need (refer to 'cash flow forecast')

20. Present financing (if applicable)
    (a) loans outstanding
        - the balance owing, repayment terms, purpose, security and status
    (b) current operating overdraft
        - the amount and security held

21. References

    (a) name of present lending institution
        – branch and type of accounts
    (b) solicitor's name
        – solicitor's address and telephone number
    (c) accountant
        – accountant's name and address and telephone number

22. Appendix

The nature of the contents of the appendices attached, if any, depends on circumstances and requirements. It is recommended that the appendices are prepared for your own benefit and reference to assist your business analysis, and to be available if the information is required. The following list is a guide only. Some of the headings described may be unavailable or unnecessary.

    (a) letter of intent
        – potential orders for client commitments
    (b) description of personal and business insurance coverage
        – include insurance policies and amount of coverage
    (c) accounts payable summary
        – include schedule of payments and total amounts owing
    (d) legal agreement
        – include a copy of contracts, leases and other documents
    (e) appraisals
        – fair market value of business property and equipment
    (f) financial statements for associated companies
        – where appropriate, a lender may require this information
    (g) copies of your brochure
    (h) testimonial letters from clients
    (i) references
    (j) sales forecast and market surveys
    (k) list of investors
    (l) credit status information
    (m) news articles about you and your business

Figure 12.2 *Opening balance sheet (new business)*

DATE: _____

NAME OF COMPANY: _____

ASSETS

Current assets
Cash and bank accounts   £ _____
Accounts receivable   £ _____
Inventory   £ _____
Prepaid rent   £ _____
Other current assets   £ _____

TOTAL CURRENT ASSETS   (A) £ _____

Fixed assets
Land and buildings   £ _____
Furniture, fixtures and equipment   £ _____
Cars   £ _____
Leasehold improvements   £ _____

Other assets   £ _____

TOTAL FIXED AND OTHER ASSETS   (B) £ _____

TOTAL ASSETS (A + B = C)   (C) £ _____

LIABILITIES

Current liabilities (debt due within
next 12 months)
Bank loans   £ _____
Loans – other   £ _____
Accounts payable   £ _____
Current portion of long-term debt   £ _____
Other current liabilities   £ _____

TOTAL CURRENT LIABILITIES   (D) £ _____

Long-term debt
Mortgages and liens payable (attach details)   £ _____
Less: current portion   £ _____
Loans from partners or stockholders (owner's equity)   £ _____
Other loans of long-term nature   £ _____

TOTAL LONG-TERM DEBT   (E) £ _____

TOTAL LIABILITIES (D + E = F)   (F) £ _____

NET WORTH (C – F = G)   (G) £ _____

TOTAL NET WORTH AND LIABILITIES (F + G = H)   (H) £ _____

Chapter 13

Selecting Business and Professional Advisers

Since you may be operating on your own, or with a few associates, you will need an extended management team to advise you in specialised areas where you lack knowledge, ability or interest. Your advisers are, in effect, your employees and associates, and should be considered an integral part of management decision-making.

Every business decision involves a legal decision or implication. Every business decision involves accounting, bookkeeping and, at times, tax considerations. The fatality rate of small businesses is high.

This chapter discusses the benefits of the effective use of business and professional advisers, how to evaluate them, and how to use their skills to your advantage.

General criteria for adviser selection

How well you select your professional and business advisers will have a direct bearing on your business success. Poor advisers or no advisers at all will almost certainly lead to your business downfall. Your main advisers are your solicitor and your accountant, followed by your bank manager. You should see at least three different people from each of these three professions before you make your selection. It is important to have the comparative assessment.

The following general guidelines should assist you in the careful search for and selection of your advisers.

Recommendations

One of the most reliable methods of finding an adviser is by a personal recommendation from your bank manager, your existing advisers or friends in business whose judgement and business sense you trust. Bank managers and business advisers who deal on a regular basis with professional advisers are in a good position to pass judgement based on their business dealings. When solicitors, accountants or bank managers refer each other, it implies a good working relationship and mutual trust. Don't rely completely on any referral; make your own cautious assessment.

Clientele

Most professional advisers have a homogeneous client base. Some advisers have many small business clients, some specialise in personal clients, while others go after corporate business. An adviser with a good base of small- to medium-size commercial clients will probably be the most appropriate for your business needs.

Fees

Fees will often vary by the size of the town in which the professional practice is operated, the size of the practice and the volume of business. You may find that advisers who charge fees in the middle range, edging towards the higher end of the scale, are often quality practitioners in great demand who are still aggressive and innovative in their business practice.

Advisers who are at the low end of the fee scale can be entrepreneurial types, but cut-rate pricing may also indicate a cut-rate, high-volume approach to business which will not suit your objectives. Low prices are sometimes an indicator of low quality, low esteem or little experience.

Very high-priced advisers tend to be more conservative, less aggressive and less willing to spend the necessary time with small business clients, as their priorities are the big firms. Fees vary and many professionals will negotiate them.

It is important to be very open when discussing fees and payment expectations.

Technical competence and industry knowledge

You must satisfy yourself that your adviser is competent in the areas of your greatest need. Ask him or her how much experience, and how comfortable, he or she is with your field.

A specific understanding of the problems, needs and issues of your type of business can enable your advisers to provide the exact assistance you require. This is different from technical skill competence. It has more to do with experience in a particular type of industry. If the adviser has provided guidance to other small business owners in similar situations, it is likely that the adviser will be able to provide you with more reliable assistance. For example, if you are a hospital consultant, a lawyer who specialises in or who is very familiar with health or hospital law could be an asset to you.

Style and personality

A critical factor in the selection of advisers, beyond simple compatibility, is style. You can have greater confidence in the aggressive adviser who takes the initiative and offers advice before you request it. This style indicates an initiator rather than a reactor, a person who anticipates and performs before matters become serious. It also indicates a creator, an entrepreneur and a person who can empathise with your problems and concerns. This kind of adviser is more likely to come up with creative solutions to problems, and be a complement to your planning function. This type of adviser will not only be a sounding board, but a true part of the management team.

Confidence

You should feel a sense of confidence when relating to your adviser, whether it be in the general sense or in dealing with a specific problem or issue. You should have a certain amount of personal compatibility with your adviser. If you don't, you will probably end up rejecting a fair amount of advice. In other words, if you do not feel that good chemistry exists between you and your adviser, seek a replacement as soon as possible. If you do not relate well to your adviser, you may hesitate to ask for advice, which could result in some poor management decisions.

Never allow your advisers to treat you in a condescending or paternalistic manner. You should consider them as equals with special knowledge offering a service in the same way that you are offering a service to your clients.

Communication

You should select an adviser who communicates well, openly and free of jargon. Your adviser should explain the necessary concepts to you so that you understand the issues involved and the decisions that have to be made. Effective communication also means that your advisers forward to you any correspondence sent or received through their offices relating to your business.

Commitment

It is important to sense that your adviser is committed to your best interests and your success. An adviser who is involved with larger, more important or higher paying clients than you may become indifferent to your needs. You should be alert to this.

Availability

It is important for your advisers to be available when you need them. You are spending time and resources to develop a relationship that will enhance your business decisions. If your adviser is frequently out of town or, in the case of a solicitor, in court on a regular basis, you may not have the immediate access you need. Of course, if the adviser is of exceptional quality and ideally suited to your type of practice, some allowances should be made.

Length of time in practice
There is naturally a correlation between the degree of expertise and length of time in practice. You should therefore ask directly how many years' experience your adviser has in the area of your needs.

Ability to aid growth
A good professional adviser will have a history of assisting growth in other clients. The adviser would be able to anticipate growth problems in advance, and provide guidance to deal with them.

Small firm versus large firm
Choosing a small or large firm is in many ways a matter of your own personal style and the type of firm you relate to most comfortably. Larger firms tend to be in the central area of town, which may involve parking problems. Their fees are higher. The larger firms may not have a small business orientation in their marketing and service priorities; although many are beginning to seek this kind of business. The larger firms do have highly specialised advisers and a resource base of associate personnel. This degree of depth may or may not be necessary in your situation. It is not uncommon in larger firms to have small business clients passed over to junior associates or trainees as the more senior advisers handle larger clients.

Smaller firms generally deal with and relate to small business entrepreneurs. Selecting an adviser in a small- or medium-size firm of three to ten people provides you with a resource base if you need it. An adviser who is a sole practitioner may be very busy, too generalised in his or her areas of practice, and lack a referral resource base within the firm.

Solicitor

There are basically two types of solicitor that you should consider as your advisers. The same person might be able to assume both roles.

You need a solicitor who specialises in small business. A solicitor who cares about small business clients assumes the same role and attitude towards your business health and survival as your doctor to your personal health.

The other type of solicitor you may need is one who specialises in contract law. You may need to have several contracts prepared depending upon the type and style of service that you are providing. You can then modify these contracts on an individual client basis. There are times when you will need to have a specialised contract made up by a solicitor or have the solicitor review and advise you on a contract that has been prepared by the client.

If your business solicitor does not have the expertise in contract law, ask if you can be referred to someone within the firm, or outside, who does. For continuity and efficiency, you want to maintain your business solicitor for all matters that don't require additional expertise. You should be able to phone your solicitor as your needs arise, and feel confident that the unique aspects of your business are known and understood.

For your protection, you should retain a solicitor before you start up your business, as there are many legal pitfalls that can be encountered. There is a temptation to save money on legal fees in the early stages of the business when cash flow is minimal. Some people do their own incorporation to save on initial start-up expenses, but then continue the saving by never obtaining legal or accounting advice, an unfortunate example of false economy and bad judgement.

Accountant

An accountant is the other essential business adviser on your management team. It is very important that you obtain a properly qualified accountant.

There are many essential services that an accountant can provide. Some of them are discussed below.

An accountant can advise on all the start-up steps of a new business, including the tax and accounting considerations of various types of business organisation. Normally, an accountant will communicate with or coordinate work with your solicitor. The accountant considers such important matters as when your financial year-end should be.

An accountant can advise on preparing a business plan for a loan application. This includes recommending the type of loan you should consider and how it is to be paid. Documents such as a profit and loss statement, a balance sheet and a financial statement can be prepared by the accountant. He or she may refer you to a bank manager, which can have a positive effect on your loan application if the bank manager knows and respects the accountant.

An accountant can advise on all aspects of tax planning and tax-related business decisions which occur from time to time as well as file your tax returns.

An accountant can advise on how to set up your office bookkeeping system. The accountant can have the bookkeeping done by someone in his or her firm, at a negotiated fee, or you can hire an independent bookkeeper. Your accountant should be able to recommend some bookkeepers.

An accountant can analyse and interpret your financial information, point out areas that need control and recommend ways of implementing the necessary change.

An accountant can coordinate your personal and business affairs and advise you on investments, tax planning and other matters.

An accountant can advise and assist you if you want to change your business or partnership into a limited company at some point. If the transfer is done correctly, you can minimise any negative tax consequences.

Bank manager

Your relationship with your bank and bank manager is your financial lifeline. The process of selecting a bank and banker is a critical one, and substantial comparative shopping is necessary in order to obtain the best combination of personality and knowledge.

Your bank should be considered in the light of specific experience with your type of business, specific reputation for taking risk and the demands that are made for security and for reporting results.

Find out the amount of the particular branch's loan approval limit. If your needs are less than the limit, the loan can be approved by the manager without further review by a higher authority. This means you only have to convince one person to approve your loan request, not additional anonymous people behind the scenes. How well your relationship develops with the manager and how successfully your loans are approved will depend largely on the factors outlined in Chapter 15 on how to obtain finance.

There are specific danger areas that can affect your bank manager's relationship with you. When the manager changes, there is always a period of risk and uncertainty. The new manager does not want to have any medium- or high-risk loans on the books to taint his or her record. During the first three or four months after a new manager takes over outstanding loans are reviewed and categorised within the criteria set by the new manager. This is the time when loans can be called in or additional security requested or interest rates increased. You should develop a personal relationship with the manager when you take out a loan. If you hear that a new manager has taken over, make a point of quickly introducing yourself and briefly discussing your business in a positive way.

Bank policies change from time to time and your type of business could be looked upon as increasing in risk. If you think the bank is concerned, prepare a realistic assessment of how you intend to deal with the situation in advance. You may have a diversified consultancy, or you may have other options available that you could explain to your bank.

If you have established a good relationship with your bank and bank manager, stay with them. Alternatively, ask your accountant and solicitor which bank and branch they recommend. This is probably one of the most effective introductions. If the bank manager has a relationship with a professional who is advising you as a client, a less impersonal relationship will exist, and there is a better chance that decisions affecting your loans and your business will be made more carefully.

Insurance and pensions

It is important to select a professional insurance broker with experience and knowledge in the areas of insurance you require. An insurance broker can have various professional qualifications, and you may wish to find out what those credentials are. You should preferably use brokers who are registered as financial advisers. Insurance is covered in more detail in Chapter 21.

Consultants

Private consultants

You may wish to approach a practising consultant for advice to assist you in your business. Apply the general criteria for adviser selection. You will want to satisfy yourself that the consultant is personally successful. If the consultant has not been successful, how can he or she possibly offer advice that will help you?

Chapter 14

Structuring and Naming the Business

Types of legal structure

There are basically three forms of legal structure: sole trader, partnership and limited company. You should seek competent legal and accounting advice before deciding on your business structure, as there could be distinct advantages or disadvantages to each, depending upon your situation.

Many consultants start out as sole traders, as that is the easiest way to start a business. If additional skills or personnel are required on a specific project, subconsultants may be retained as independent contractors by the sole trader.

In a partnership of two or more consultants problems of working together could arise which could lead to the dissolution of the partnership. In the field of consultancy, in particular, a healthy ego is essential to sell yourself and your skills. Because of this, conflict may occur when two or more consultants share joint decision-making but have individual dreams and goals.

Forming a company is a third option. The company can be owned by just one person (similar to a sole trader) or two or more people (similar to a partnership).

The next section of this chapter discusses the factors that you and your professional advisers should examine when making a decision about your business structure.

Advantages and disadvantages of different types of structure

Sole trader
If you are working on your own as a sole practitioner you can set up in business as a sole trader. This is the simplest form of structure.

Advantages
Ease of formation. There is less formality and few legal restrictions associated with establishing yourself as a sole trader. You can start almost

immediately. There are no complex forms to complete and no documentation required between yourself and any other party. All you need to do is to inform the Inland Revenue for income tax and the Department of Social Security for National Insurance contribution purposes. If you are providing financial advice or operating a form of employment agency you will also need a government licence.

Cost. Registering the business and obtaining licences involve minimal costs. There are no partnership or corporate agreements required because you are the sole owner. Legal fees are reduced accordingly.

Lack of complexity. Operating as a sole trader is straightforward. Unlike other forms of business there is little government control and, accordingly, fewer reports are required to be filed with government agencies and departments. The owner and the business are taxed as one.

Decision-making process. Decisions are made exclusively by the sole owner, who has complete authority and freedom to move. The owner does not have to obtain approval from partners or shareholders or a board of directors.

Sole ownership of profits. The sole trader does not have to share the profits with anyone. The profits generated by the business belong to one person. The sole owner decides how and when the money will come out of the business.

Ease of terminating/sale of business. Apart from legal responsibilities to employees, creditors or perhaps clients, you can sell the business or close it down at your will.

Flexibility. You are able to respond quickly to business needs in day-to-day management decisions as governed by various laws and common sense.

Disadvantages
Unlimited liability. The sole trader's personal assets, such as house, property, car and investments, are liable to be seized if necessary to pay for outstanding debts or liabilities. As mentioned earlier, the proprietor and the business are deemed to be one and the same in law.

Less financing capacity. It is more difficult for a sole trader to borrow money than for a partnership with various partners or a limited company with a number of major shareholders. A lender, when looking for security and evidence of outside resources, can turn to other people connected with the business rather than just the one person operating as a sole trader. A partnership or company can give an investor some form of equity position, which is not available with a sole trader.

Unstable duration of business. The business might be crippled or terminated upon the illness or death of the owner. If there is no one appropriate to take over the business, it may have to be sold or liquidated. Such an unplanned action may result in a loss.

Sole decision-making. In partnerships or companies, generally there is shared decision-making or at least input. With a sole trader, just one person is involved, and if that person lacks business ability or experience, poor decision-making can cause the business to suffer.

Partnership
A partnership is usually defined as an association of two or more people to carry on a business in common with a view to making a profit. The partnership is created by a contract, either verbal or written, between the individual parties.

Advantages
Ease of formation. Legal formalities and expenses in forming a partnership are few compared to incorporating.

Pride of ownership and direct rewards. Pride of ownership generates personal motivation and identification with the business. The profit motive could be reinforced with more people having a vested interest.

Availability of more capital. A partnership can pool the funds of a number of people compared to a sole trader who has only his or her own resources to draw upon, unless loans are obtained.

Combination of expertise and talent. Two or more partners, by combining their energies and talents, can often be successful where one person alone would fail. This is particularly true if the business demands a variety of talents such as technical knowledge, sales ability and financial skills. It is important that working partners bring complementary skills to the business, thereby reducing the workload of each partner.

Flexibility. A partnership may be relatively more flexible in the decision-making process than a company, but less so than a sole proprietorship.

Relative freedom of government control and special taxation. Compared with a company, a partnership is relatively free from restrictions and bureaucratic red tape.

Disadvantages

Unlimited liability. The major disadvantage of a partnership is the unlimited liability. This unlimited liability is much more serious than for a sole trader because all the partners are individually *and* collectively liable for all the debts and liabilities of the partnership. Each partner's personal assets are liable to be seized if necessary to pay for outstanding business debts.

Unstable duration of business. Any change in the partnership automatically ends the legal entity. Changes could include the death of a partner, or the admission or withdrawal of a partner. In each case, if the business is to continue, a new partnership agreement must be written.

Management difficulties. As mentioned, when more than one owner assumes responsibility for business management there is a possibility that differences of style, priorities, philosophy and other factors will arise. If these differences become serious disputes and are unresolvable, the partnership may have to be terminated, with all the financial and personal trauma involved. It is difficult for future partners to foresee whether or not personalities and methods of operating will clash.

Relative difficulty in obtaining large sums of capital. This is particularly true of long-term financing when compared to a company.

Partnership agreement problems. The larger a partnership becomes, the more complex the written agreement has to be to protect the rights and identify the responsibilities of each partner. This can result in additional administration and legal costs.

Difficulty of disposing of partnership interest. To withdraw capital from the business requires approval from all the other partners. This takes time and involves legal and administrative expenses.

Partnership agreement

A partnership agreement (sometimes called articles of partnership) is absolutely necessary in a partnership relationship. The agreement normally outlines the contribution of each partner in the business, whether financial, material or managerial. In general, it defines the roles of the partners in the business relationship. See the checklist in Table 14.1.

If you are considering a partnership relationship, complete the checklist headings and then see your solicitor and accountant. By the time you have completed the checklist with your prospective partner, one or both of you may have second thoughts.

Table 14.1. *Checklist of articles in a partnership agreement*

1. Name, purpose and location of partnership
2. Duration of agreement
3. Names and character of partners (general or limited, active or silent)
4. Financial contribution by partners (at inception, at later date)
5. Role of individual partners in business management
6. Authority (authority of partner in conduct of business)
7. Nature and degree of each partner's contribution to firm's consulting services
8. Business expenses (how handled)
9. Separate debts
10. Signing of cheques
11. Division of profits and losses
12. Books, records and method of accounting
13. Withdrawals or salaries
14. Absence and disability
15. Death of a partner (dissolution and winding up)
16. Rights of continuing partner
17. Employee management
18. Sale of partnership interest
19. Release of debts
20. Settlement of disputes, arbitration
21. Additions, alterations or modifications to partnership agreement
22. Non-competition in the event of departure

Limited company

A limited company is a legal entity, with or without share capital, which can be established by one or more individuals or other legal entities. It exists separate and distinct from these individuals or other legal entities. A limited company has all the rights and responsibilities of a person with the exception of those rights that can only be exercised by a natural person.

Advantages
Limited liability of shareholders. Shareholders' personal assets are separate

from the business and cannot be seized to pay for outstanding business debts incurred by the corporation. There are exceptions, dealing primarily with the issue of fraud.

Flexibility for tax planning. Various tax advantages are available to corporations that are not available to partnerships or sole traders. Tax planning must be undertaken with the help of a professional accountant.

Corporate management flexibility. The owner or owners can be active in the management of the business to any desired degree. Agents, officers and directors with specified authority can be appointed to manage the business. Employees can be given stock options to share in the ownership, which can increase incentive and interest.

Financing more readily available. Investors find it more attractive to invest in a company with its limited liability than to invest in a business whose unlimited liability could involve them to an extent greater than the amount of the investment. Long-term financing from lending institutions is more available since lenders may use both corporate assets and personal guarantees as security.

Continual existence of corporation. A company continues to exist and operate regardless of the changes in the shareholders. Death of a shareholder does not discontinue the life of the company. Continual existence is also an effective device for building and retaining goodwill.

Ownership is readily transferable. It is a relatively simple procedure to transfer ownership by share transfer unless there are corporate restrictions to the contrary.

Draw on expertise and skills of more than one individual. This feature is the same concept as in a partnership, where more partners (shareholders) contribute diverse talents. However, a company is not required to have more than one shareholder.

Disadvantages
Extensive government regulations. There are more regulations affecting a company than a sole trader or partnership. Companies must report to all levels of government.

Manipulation. Minority shareholders are potentially in a position to be exploited by the decisions of the majority of the company.

Expense. It is more expensive to establish and operate a company because of the additional documents and forms that are required compared to a sole trader or partnership.

Choice

As a generalisation, a small business is probably better off in tax terms being started as a sole trader or partnership. A mature, profitable business may, however, be better off by being incorporated.

The choice between setting up as a sole trader or as a partnership is largely dependent on individual preferences and circumstances. Consultants often start as sole practitioners and, when they are established, form a partnership with one or more congenial people. Quite often, two or three people who have worked together in a normal business or in a consultancy decide that they want to 'put up their plate' and become a consultancy partnership. Alternatively, two people can get together with an idea for a consultancy niche and set up in partnership.

Spouses are often involved, either as employees of the other spouse or in partnership with them. Sometimes a consultant sets up as a sole trader and employs his or her spouse at a fixed salary (and there may be tax advantages in doing so, although PAYE and National Insurance contributions have to be administered). At a later stage it may be considered advantageous from an operational, financial or tax point of view to set up a partnership.

Whatever approach you adopt you should get advice from your accountant on the financial and tax implications and from your solicitor on legal matters.

Selecting a name

Selecting your name is an important decision both from an image and a legal perspective. It is essential to be aware of the implications of selecting your name to make it correct from the outset.

Many consultants do business under their own names, for example, 'David Jones, Management Consultant'. The business card and letterhead would also show the address and telephone number and a brief description of the service. The description could read, for example, 'Research studies and project management'.

Many consultants prefer to use their own name because they are offering a personal service and promoting and selling themselves. The drawback of using your name is that it implies a one-person operation; this could cause a client to doubt your capacity to complete a project if you are ill or injured. For this reason, and by personal choice, some consultants prefer to use the phrase, 'David Jones Associates, Management Consultants'. This implies a business with more than one person and a resource base of skilled consultants.

Many consultants contract with subconsultants as required, depending upon the job project. This cuts down on overheads, provides depth and flexibility, and expands consulting contract opportunities. Your network should include both management consultants with complementary skills and management consultants who are practising in the same field. You can include them as required in an assignment proposal as associates.

It is important to describe the nature of the services you are offering, and not limit the future development of your consulting service. For example, if you are a hospital consultant, you may not want to state on your letterhead or business card 'specialising in personnel development' if you could receive other spin-off consulting work outside the limits of description of personnel development. Don't use the word 'freelance', as it may not project the professional image you want to create.

Some consultants prefer not to use their own name in the firm's name for a number of reasons. One reason is that the consultant does not want an employer to be aware that a consulting business is being operated part time. Another reason is that if goodwill is developed under a company's name rather than an individual's, a higher price might be obtained if the consulting practice is sold.

Chapter 15

Raising Finance

Your start-up expenses as a consultant could be anything from £2000 to £10,000 or more. In addition, you will have a marketing budget and will want to draw an adequate income for yourself from the practice. But you will have to face the fact that during your first year or two you will be establishing yourself and cannot therefore rely on reaching your full earning potential. You may need funds to fill this gap, the size of which will depend on your earning capacity, the costs of running the practice, the effectiveness of your tax-planning procedures and how much you want for yourself. It is not unusual for consultants to earn fees for only a very small proportion of their available time in their first year. Allowing for the costs of running a practice as a sole trader from home and of supporting themselves and, possibly, their families, the deficit in the first year might be as much as £20,000 or more. You must, of course, establish this figure more precisely with the help of your accountant while preparing your business plan, and this will indicate how much extra finance you will need, if any, to get you started and take you to your break-even point.

It is necessary to be realistic at this stage. Don't set over-optimistic targets for fees. If you are starting from scratch and are not fortunate enough to have an existing portfolio of clients waiting to snap you up, you might well find it difficult to charge yourself out for more than 25 per cent of your time in the first year. Now is the time to assess what you think you *might* need so that finance will be available to tide you over short-term cash flow problems until you can fully realise your earning capacity.

If you do need to raise finance the following are the main ways of doing so:

- Bank borrowing
- Private loans
- Local authorities
- The Enterprise Allowance Scheme.

These are summarised below. For more detailed information read *Working for Yourself* by Godfrey Golzen (Kogan Page, 10th edition, 1988) or the other books on setting up a business referred to in the Bibliography, page 228.

Bank borrowing

This is the most common method of raising finance for a small concern. The banks are in the business of lending money and your manager will be helpful if he or she feels that your proposition is viable.

Bank managers have three main criteria which they use in evaluating applications for business finance:

1. Will their money be secure? Banks will probably ask for security in the shape of tangible items such as fixed assets within the business, or shares and other assets belonging to the owners in their private capacity in a ratio which may be as high as 1:1.
2. Is your firm likely to have an inflow of enough liquid assets to enable the bank's money to be recalled if necessary?
3. Will you be able to make profitable use of the money and pay the interest without difficulty?

To a certain extent bank managers go on personal impressions and what they know of the applicant's previous business experience. But a thorough approach is required to ensure that they accept your proposition as a good business risk. When you are starting any business, and especially a consultancy business, you may not have much more than hopes for the future to offer. But you must attempt to quantify these hopes and produce a realistic and convincing cash flow budget.

The best medium for presenting a case for finance is your business plan, as discussed in Chapter 12. The banks have kits which show you how to prepare them and Godfrey Golzen has suggested that the salient points a bank will want to see covered are:

- Your business experience;
- Your existing assets and liabilities;
- The product or service you are proposing to offer, the geographical market for it and how you propose to reach it;
- The likely demand for it – ie whether it is continuing and to what extent it is seasonal or susceptible to technological obsolescence;
- Competition. Where it is and how you propose to counter it by means of price, service etc;
- Requirements for and likely costs of premises and/or equipment;
- How much of your own money you are proposing to put in;

- The amount of finance required and what it is going to be used for;
- What security you are able to offer;
- Cash flow and profit and loss forecast for the first 12 months.

Private loans

You might have friends or relatives who would be prepared to lend you money or guarantee an overdraft. But such loans or arrangements can be fraught with difficulties and end beautiful friendships or create family rifts. If you must follow this route, ensure that a solicitor draws up a loan agreement setting out rates of interest, the period over which the loan is repayable and the circumstances under which it can be withdrawn.

Local authorities

Some local authorities have funds available to help business development. The 14 London boroughs, for example, run Greater London Enterprise for this purpose. The funds may be used for grants or to make loans. But the main purpose of these bodies is to create employment opportunities and a one-person consultancy firm may not be attractive to them.

The Enterprise Allowance Scheme

The government's Enterprise Allowance Scheme has emerged as the most accessible and widely used of all grant sources. The target for the scheme is 100,000 entrants a year.

If you have been unemployed for eight weeks, have a viable idea for starting your own business and are prepared to put £1000 of your own money into it (this can be a loan), you can get a grant of £40 a week for 52 weeks. Applications for an Enterprise Allowance are vetted by local Jobcentres and they usually take a very broad view of the criteria for eligibility, except that you need to be receiving unemployment or supplementary benefit when you apply. You do, however, have to put in a minimum working week of 36 hours, though you are entitled to four weeks' holiday and a maximum of eight weeks off for illness. A very important point to bear in mind, though, is that you must apply for your Enterprise Allowance *before* you start trading.

Chapter 16

Setting Up the Office

Selecting an office

Most consultants begin by operating from their own homes. As the practice grows the decision might be made to move into an office.

Normally, consultants go to the client's office, but occasionally clients wish to meet the consultant at the consultant's place of business.

Working from home

There are several advantages to operating from home. You save money on services, travel and rent. The stress of commuting to work is reduced. You are able to deduct from income tax the portion of your home you are using for business purposes. (The tax deductions you can use when you have a home office are covered in Chapter 19.)

Being close to the family is an important consideration for some consultants.

There are also disadvantages to working from home. You may be distracted by your family during the working day. Your presence may be distracting to your family. The mix of home and office dynamics could negatively affect your private life. You could turn into a workaholic because of the proximity of your office. Your home might be distant from your clients' offices, which would make it difficult for your clients to visit you. If clients come to your home occasionally, you want your home to present a positive impression so as not to detract from your professional image. Your home address on your stationery and business card could present a questionable image to prospective clients who may wonder about your business competence. Clients may view you as a freelance, and be more likely to question your fees.

Because of the limitations of working from your home, you may wish to use an accommodation address which will forward mail and provide a telephone answering service. It helps your image if the address is prestigious but, of course, it will cost you more. The Yellow Pages list suppliers of accommodation addresses.

Having a personalised telephone answering service, as provided by British Telecom, connected to your telephone at home allows you the freedom of knowing your telephone calls are being handled in a professional manner whether you are at home or out making calls. By keeping the answering service informed of your schedule for the day, your callers will receive the appropriate response and know when the call might be returned.

If possible, avoid using an answering machine; they don't present a professional image, callers receive the impression that you are a one-person operation (which, of course, you are), and you may be perceived as a freelance, which has a negative connotation for some people.

Office outside home

You may wish to have an office outside your home when circumstances and finances justify it. Having your own office address increases credibility and stature when dealing with clients or prospective clients. Studies have shown that consultants are able to collect higher fees for performing the same work when operating from an office.

When considering an office location, factors such as expense, image of business address, your proximity to clients and referral possibilities should be examined.

Try to look at your long-range goals over two years and imagine what your office needs might be. It is costly to pay for new office stationery and other start-up costs and several moves may create an image of instability.

Office sharing arrangement

You may wish to look for an office with complementary professional or business tenants and prospective business clients. You have your own office and generally supply your own personal office furniture, but the rent expenses of the overall office and the receptionist's salary are shared on a proportional basis by the tenants. The secretarial expenses are negotiated depending upon use.

If you do seek out a pooling arrangement, try to have a minimal notice period to leave the premises. You may wish to leave because of expansion, inability to pay the rent or personality conflicts. It is fairly common to have a three-month notice provision. Make sure that the terms of your rental relationship are in writing and signed by the necessary parties before you begin your relationship.

As a general caution, avoid sharing space with a client. You could fall out or the client could attempt to use your time for free or look on you as staff.

Sharing same private office

Two or more people may use the same office space. The parties agree on the costs of furnishing the office, unless it was already furnished, and an agreement would be worked out in terms of the hours and days of use. Costs of this arrangement are negotiated on a per use basis.

Office rental package

There are firms in the business of renting packaged office space. There can be anywhere from 5 to 50 tenants or more. Each tenant has a private office, and there is a common reception area.

The office package arrangement is a good source of potential contacts for networking or prospective clients, depending upon the mix of the tenants.

Frequently, telephone answering and office furniture are included in the package price as well as a nominal number of hours of secretarial time per month. The rental arrangement may involve a minimum two- or three-month notice to vacate, or a six-month or one-year lease arrangement. Prices and terms of various office package arrangements may be negotiable if there is competition in that market-place.

There are several other advantages of an office package arrangement. Other services are often available which save you considerable money on staff and equipment. These include:

- Street mailing address – not a post office box number;
- Postage metered mail for prompt delivery and a professional appearance;
- Typing or word processing – a variety of typestyles available on modern equipment for letters, reports, invoices, statements etc;
- Word processing services with the advantages of speed, efficiency and storage and retrieval capacity;
- Dictaphone transcription;
- Secretarial services, including letter composition and editing using correct business language and form;
- Photocopying – a copier with various features including collating could be available to produce quality copies on your letterhead, transparencies or address labels;
- Telex service;
- Fax service.

Occasional office
You can rent a boardroom or an office for as short a time as an hour, or half a day or a day. The cost is negotiable. The occasional office space can be found through office rental package services described earlier (page 138). Some firms stipulate that you must have a telephone answering or professional identity package arrangement with them before you are able to rent occasional space.

Leased space
Leasing space does have its disadvantages, and it is most important that you consult your accountant and a competent solicitor familiar with commercial leases before signing anything. You should shop around for space to make sure you have the best arrangement for your needs and to assist you in negotiating.

Some of the clauses to be wary of when you are considering a lease include restrictions on your ability to sublet or assign your lease, liabilities and duties of the landlord and tenant, the use you intend for the premises, limitations on alterations or improvements to the premises, acceleration clauses in case of default, and a requirement for your personal guarantee if you are doing business as a company. Always check on rent review provisions.

If you are still interested in signing a lease, try to negotiate as many attractive features as possible. All leases are negotiable and there are no standard clauses. Your solicitor can advise you properly and possibly negotiate the lease on your behalf.

Some tips on negotiating your lease include:

(a) Rather than negotiating a three-year lease, for example, try to negotiate a one-year lease with two additional one-year options. This way you minimise the risk in case you cannot afford the lease or in case you need to expand or the premises are otherwise unsuitable for your needs.

(b) Consider offering the last two or three months rent as a deposit. If you default the lease and leave before the end of the term, the deposit monies go to the landlord, and you are free of any further liability.

(c) Put in the lease that alterations or improvements you intend to make will be at the landlord's expense.

(d) Attempt to get the first few months free of rent as an incentive for you to lease the premises.

(e) Try to get out of paying the last month's security deposit rent, if possible. If it is not possible, try to negotiate with the landlord to pay you interest at a fixed rate on the security deposit money.

Another factor in leasing space is the additional expense for furniture and equipment for your office and reception area, plus the additional costs of a secretary or receptionist. All these additional costs have to be carefully considered to ensure there is sufficient cash flow to justify the commitment.

Never enter into a lease agreement without consulting your solicitor.

Equipping an office

Equipping an office is not too expensive if you buy second-hand furniture. You can obtain good used business furniture from bankruptcy sales, auction sales or through the classified section in the newspaper. The type and quality of furniture that you select will naturally relate to your type of consulting clientele and the image that you want to project.

There are certain basic things you need for your office, including desk, chairs, tables, lamps, bookcases, filing cabinet, typewriter or, preferably, word processor, calculator, telephone answering device (optional), tape recorder (as a dictaphone, to record meetings, to record consulting or marketing ideas), and card file and/or address file.

Additionally, you might need a fax machine (these are increasingly being used) and a photocopier.

Office supplies

The basic supplies you need include business cards, letterhead stationery and printed envelopes, brochures, records for bookkeeping, invoices, filing folders and various types of calendars.

Business stationery, cards, envelopes

Your business stationery is very important as it represents you, your image and your business. It should present a professional and conservative image. It should state your name, your business name, the type of consulting (if applicable) address, post code, telephone number and fax number.

All your stationery should correspond with the format and image of your business card. Choose a good quality paper stock. Buy blank pages of your letter stock so that your second page will match the colour of the first. Neutral colours, such as beige, ivory or white, create a professional impression. You have a choice between litho (flat) or thermo (raised) ink. The thermo's raised, glossy appearance creates a richer effect. The cost of raised letter is not much more than flat, but extra time is required for printing. As the printing business is very competitive, be sure to compare rates.

Some consultants prefer to have a logo on their business card. Ask a graphic artist to design it and, if you can afford it, to design all your business and promotional material.

Brochures
Depending upon the type of consulting practice that you have and the nature of clientele you wish to attract, brochures may be part of your marketing plan. Naturally, brochures are less expensive by quantity. You may choose to engage the services of a promotional copy-writer to assist you in preparing the text for a brochure that will effectively outline the services you provide for your specific clientele or market. You can also use the services of a design consultancy to develop your 'house style' or 'corporate image', and to design your brochure as well as your letterhead and logo, if any. For printing, check for competitive rates and allow yourself considerable lead time to obtain the best rate. One colour ink on coloured stock is less expensive than two inks and can be just as effective.

Record-keeping documents, invoices and file folders
These items are necessary for the orderly maintenance of projects, systems and good business management. The types of records you should keep are outlined in Chapter 17.

Diaries
For recording appointments, telephone calls and deadlines you should have a desk diary, a wall planner, and a daily diary that you carry with you. The time that you spend on assignments must be recorded in detail for proper invoicing and for your protection in the event of a dispute.

Personnel

Secretarial staff
Most consultants starting up do not have the workload or cash flow to justify employing a secretary. Some consultants prefer to type the documents and correspondence themselves, but even if you are a good typist, you will make more money consulting or finding new clients than you will typing. Some consultants ask a member of the family to do the typing, but this can create strains on the relationship.

It is far more cost-effective and practical to 'rent' a secretary. In some cases, the typing costs related to an assignment file can be billed directly to the client in addition to your fees. You then have verification from the typing agency if there is any question on your account.

Find a professional typing agency that offers temporary services. Ask how much lead time is required, what the turn-around time is and what other services they offer. Interview several agencies and ask to see sample copies of their reports, newsletters and correspondence so that you can judge the professional quality of the work.

It is essential that word processing services are available. As a consultant, you will be producing large quantities of material that require neat, clean and correctly styled typing. A word processor can produce this quality, and store your contracts, proposals, standard letters, reports and mailing lists for retrieval.

A professional secretarial agency can also look after all your correspondence and document needs including preparing invoices and reminder letters for your outstanding accounts. You can ask the agency if one staff member will work on your file so that person will become familiar with your style. A dictaphone tape for transcription is a considerable benefit in terms of consistency and saving time when one person becomes accustomed to your method of dictating.

Retaining other consultants

Employing another consultant as an independent contractor, in other words, a subconsultant, is a common technique to reduce overheads and increase your resource base and efficiency. There are times when you might need specialised skills or additional help to be able to satisfy a potential client contract. Try to develop a network of consultants you can call on when needed. Many consultants take on projects they could not complete themselves and subcontract portions to another consultant.

It is important to maintain your position with your client as the main source of information and communication. Your client need not know that you have subcontracted out a part of the job, but it often adds credibility to your proposal if you have additional expertise available to allocate to the assignment.

Selecting a telephone system

Your telephone, in many ways, is your lifeline to a successful consulting practice. Many consultants start out using their home telephone number and a telephone answering device, but there are problems with this. Inexpensive alternatives exist. The important consideration is the impression your telephone system gives your clients or prospective clients and how effectively you receive incoming messages.

142

A separate telephone at home

Many consultants operating from home prefer to have a separate line for their consulting practice. This saves the frustration of having children answer your phone or family members tying up the line with their personal calls.

Answering service

You may wish to have an office number that does not go to your home, but terminates at an answering service. Your answering service could then phone you at home (if those were your instructions) and advise you of a phone message.

Voicebank

Voicebank is a British Telecom messaging service. Subscribers are allocated a separate Voicebank number which they can phone and record their personal message. This is relayed to callers who leave their messages which can be accessed by dialling the Voicebank 'mailbank'. Up to ten callers at once can call on the Voicebox number. In addition to this recording service subscribers can send messages to other subscribers automatically through the 'mailbox' system.

Fax

Facsimile machines are now frequently installed in businesses in the UK and Europe. Communications with clients can be improved immensely by faxing messages or data, and if you are getting in touch frequently with clients it may well pay you to invest in a fax machine.

Telex

Telex is particularly useful for sending messages where fax is not available, especially in areas outside Europe where postal delays are likely. It is not necessary to have your own telex machine. British Telecom have telex centres which provide a perfectly good service.

Chapter 17

Record Systems

The record systems you require will fall into four categories:

- Accounting records
- Client records
- Assignment records
- Consultant records.

Accounting records

Purpose
Your accounting system exists to help you control the business. It records receipts and payments, forecasts and monitors cash flows, shows the profit or loss you are making and defines the assets and liabilities of the business in financial terms.

At the end of each accounting period you will need to be able to supply figures for your own purposes and as required by the Inland Revenue and Customs and Excise covering:

(a) Takings – fee earnings and VAT listed separately;

(b) Expenditures – covering separate items such as rent, rates, lighting, insurance, motor vehicle, travel, subsistence, accommodation when away from home on business, salaries of employees (gross before tax and National Insurance contributions), employer's share of National Insurance contributions, stationery and postage and telephone – VAT payments to be accounted for separately;

(c) Amounts owed to you by clients at the accounting dates, showing the total and the amounts owed by each debtor;

(d) Amounts owed by you to suppliers at the accounting date, showing the total and the amount owed to each creditor;

(e) Private money introduced into the business, showing the amount and origin;

(f) The amount of any drawings or cash taken from the business for your own use;

(g) The amount of any cheques drawn on the business bank account for any private purpose.

Basic financial accounting records

The basic financial accounting records consist of evidence of business transactions such as invoices to clients (accounts receivable), bills from suppliers (accounts payable), payments to employees, petty cash vouchers, bank statements etc. Your accountant will advise you on what books of account you should keep and will, for a fee, keep them for you; or you can employ a part-time bookkeeper.

If you want to keep it simple and do it yourself the basic account records you should maintain are as follows:

1. *Cash book.* This records and itemises all incomes and expenditures, as in the example given in Figure 17.1. You may wish to record minor transactions in a petty cash book and transfer summaries periodically to the main cash book.
2. *Client accounts.* A summary for each client of the state of their accounts showing invoices presented and payments received of fees and expenses. An example is given in Figure 17.2.
3. *Payroll accounts.* Records of salary payments to any employees together with the records required for PAYE and National Insurance.

In addition you should, of course, file copies of invoices, receipts, bank statements, credit card accounts and paying-in slips, and keep used cheque books.

You can find various types of accounts books at stationery shops. Some are for recording all transactions as they occur, and they contain simple printed instructions to help you to draw up annual accounts from the daily records. Other account books are ruled into columns which you can head according to your needs.

More detailed financial records

If the business is big or complex enough to need more detailed records, the 'books of original entry' or 'journals' you can maintain include:

● a *sales journal* registering all sales by numbered invoice;
● a *cash receipts journal* which records all the money coming into the business (often combined with the sales journal as a sales and cash receipts journal);

- an *accounts receivable or sales ledger* which contains separate sheets for each client and records fees and expenses invoiced to them, and a *control account* which records in total all sales;
- an *accounts payable journal or purchase ledger* which records invoices for purchases, the amount and date and when the invoice has to be paid;
- a *cash disbursements journal* which records daily all cash outlays for purchases, expenses, payroll, cash withdrawals and loan payments;
- a *payroll journal* which records salary payments, deductions (PAYE, National Insurance, pension contributions etc);
- an *assets register* which lists and values all capital assets such as freehold buildings;
- a *general ledger* which is the final book entry – entries from the preceding journals and ledgers are listed in the general ledger which is used for preparing financial statements and management accounts.

Your accountant will advise you on the extent to which you need to keep more complex financial records. Much of the system can, of course, be computerised. There are plenty of software packages designed for the small business.

Management accounts

Management accounts summarise how the business is performing in financial terms. They provide invaluable help in planning and controlling the business. They also provide the information required by the Inland Revenue. The data recorded in the management accounts are derived from the financial accounts.

The main management accounts you should keep are:

- The *profit and loss account* as illustrated in Figure 17.3 which summarises income and expenditure over a period and records on the 'bottom line' the outcome in terms of profit or loss;
- The *cash flow statement and forecast* as illustrated in Figures 17.4 and 17.5 which records cash flows into and out of the business, sets out opening and closing balances over a period, and forecasts future cash flows and balances;
- The *budget*, as illustrated in Figure 17.6, which sets out forecast and actual sales, overheads and profit over the year and is reviewed at regular intervals so that differences between actuals and budget can be analysed and action taken to correct adverse variances.

In addition, if you have physical assets and money invested in the business you will need to keep a balance sheet as illustrated in Figure 17.7. This is essential if you are a limited company.

Client records

Client records should consist of:

1. A *new client record sheet* – see Figure 17.8
2. An *assignment record sheet* for each client – see Figure 17.9
3. The *client account summary sheet* – see Figure 17.2.

Assignment records

It is essential to control the progress of assignments by comparing actual achievements and time spent against the programme and budget included in the proposal. It is also important to record the time spent by consultants on each section of the assignment, as well as the expenses they incur, as a basis for preparing bills. These records can be invaluable if a client queries an account. In these circumstances you need written evidence that the specified amount of time was spent carrying out work which the client had agreed should be done when the proposal was approved.

The records you need for this purpose are:

1. An *assignment diary* to be completed weekly by the consultant on the assignment. If there is more than one consultant each consultant completes his or her own diary. The diary records the activities carried out during the week, cross-referenced to the proposal, the time spent on each of them and progress against budget. It also records any expenses incurred on the client's behalf. The comments section is for any remarks the consultant wants to make about the work that has been done – problems such as the possibility of an overrun or opportunities for further work (see Figure 17.10).
2. The *assignment control sheet* which lists the activities to be carried out during the assignment, giving the budgeted time for each one and the programmed completion date. The time spent on any activity is entered weekly against the budget for that week. The total time to date allocated to the activity is recorded for comparison with the total time budget. A note is also made of whether the activity has been completed (see Figure 17.11).

Consultant records

There are four types of consultant records:

1. The *consultant's brief and budget.* This is particularly useful if there is more than one consultant on the assignment. It provides an overall brief to the consultant on what he or she is expected to do and

achieve. It also sets out the programme and time budget for the consultant, listing each activity and stating how much time per week and in total should be spent on it, and when it should be completed (see Figure 17.12).

2. The *weekly time sheet*. This is completed by yourself and any other consultants employed by you. It is a vital record of how much time consultants are charging to clients. It provides the data needed to calculate utilisation rates and it analyses non-chargeable time under various headings such as conducting surveys and preparing proposals, practice development, product development and training (see Figure 17.13).

3. The *monthly summary time sheet*. This summarises for you and any other consultants the total chargeable and non-chargeable time and shows utilisation rates (see Figure 17.14).

4. The *loading sheet*. This shows the amount of time which has been committed to assignments over a future period. It highlights future utilisation problems and can help in loading consultant time on new assignments (see Figure 17.15).

Figure 17.1. *Basic cash book record sheet*

		Income						Expenditure				
Date of invoice	Invoice no.	Date paid	Details[1]	Amount[2] £	VAT £	Total[3] £	Date	Invoice no.	Method[4] of payment	Details[5]	Amount[2] £	VAT £	Total[3] £

Notes: 1. Enter client's name, whether for fees or expenses, and period for which fees/expenses have been invoiced.

2. Excluding VAT, where applicable.

3. Including VAT, where applicable.

4. Cash, cheque no. or credit card.

5. State name of client to whom expense is to be charged, where applicable.

Figure 17.2. *Client account summary sheet*

Client . . . .

Assignment start date . . . . Assignment end date . . . .

Total estimated fees £ . . . .

Payment arrangements . . . .

Invoice date	Invoice no.	Date paid	Details	Fees			Expenses	Total to date		
				Amount excluding VAT	VAT	Total		Fees excluding VAT	VAT	Expenses

Figure 17.3. *Profit and loss account*

	This month			Year to date		
	Budget £	Actual £	Variance £	Budget £	Actual £	Variance £
Income Fees Other Total income A						
Marketing/sales expenses Promotional Travel/subsistence Proposal costs Other Total marketing/ sales expenses B						
Gross profit (A — B) C						

Overheads
Salaries
Other staff costs
  (Nat. Ins. etc)
Proprietor/partner drawings
Lighting, heating,
  telephone
Rent and rates
Office expenses and
  supplies
Repairs and renewals
Professional fees
  (solicitor, accountant,
  etc)
Secretarial/computing
  services
Vehicle costs
Travel
Entertaining
Insurance
Loan/Lease costs
Bank interest and charges
Bad debts
Other
Total overheads D						

Net profit (C — D) E						
Net profit % $\left(\frac{E}{A}\right)$ (E/A x 100)						

Figure 17.4. *Monthly cash flow statement*

Cash flow for month ending	Budget £ £	Actual £ £
Balance at beginning of month		
Add:		
Receipts: fee income		
other income		
sundry receipts	———	———
Less:		
Salaries		
Other payments to or for staff		
Proprietor/partner drawings		
Lighting, heating, telephone		
Rent and rates		
Office expenses and supplies		
Repairs		
Other purchases (not capitalised)		
Capital expenditure		
Professional fees		
Secretarial/computing services		
Vehicle costs		
Travel		
Entertaining		
Insurance		
Loan/lease costs		
PAYE		
VAT		
Others (specify)	———	———
Balance at end of month		

Figure 17.5. *Cash flow budget and forecast for year*

Cash flow budget and forecast for year ending		Balance at beginning of month £	Add receipts* £	Less payments* £	Balance at end of month £
January	Budget				
	Actual				
February	Budget				
	Actual				
March	Budget				
	Actual				
April	Budget				
	Actual				
May	Budget				
	Actual				
June	Budget				
	Actual				
July	Budget				
	Actual				
August	Budget				
	Actual				
September	Budget				
	Actual				
October	Budget				
	Actual				
November	Budget				
	Actual				
December	Budget				
	Actual				

*Detailed in monthly cash flow report.

153

Figure 17.6. *Annual budget*

		Jan	Feb	March	April	May	June	July	Aug	Sept	Oct	Nov	Dec
Income													
Fees													
Other													
Total income	A												
Marketing/sales expenses													
Promotional													
Travel/subsistence													
Proposal costs													
Other													
Total marketing/sales expenses	B												
Gross profit (A — B)	C												
Overheads													
Salaries													
Other staff costs (Nat. Ins. etc)													
Proprietor/partner drawings													
Lighting, heating, telephone													
Rent and rates													
Office expenses and supplies													
Repairs and renewals													
Professional fees (solicitor, accountant etc)													

Budget for year ending............

Figure 17.6. *Annual budget – continued*

		Budget for year ending											
		Jan	Feb	March	April	May	June	July	Aug	Sept	Oct	Nov	Dec
Overheads – continued													
Secretarial/computing services													
Vehicle costs													
Travel													
Entertaining													
Insurance													
Loan/lease costs													
Bank interest and charges													
Bad debts													
Other													
Total overheads	D												
Net profit (C—D)	E												
Net profit % ($\frac{E}{A} \times 100$)													

Figure 17.7. *Balance sheet*

```
Date: _____

Name of company: _____

                     ASSETS

Current assets                                    £
   Cash and bank accounts                    _____
   Accounts receivable                       _____
   Inventory                                 _____
   Prepaid rent                              _____
   Other current assets                      _____
Total current assets                    (A)  _____

Fixed assets
   Land and buildings                        _____
   Furniture, fixtures and equipment         _____
   Vehicles                                  _____
   Leasehold improvements                    _____
Other assets                                 _____
Total fixed and other assets            (B)  _____
Total assets (A + B = C)                (C)  _____

                   LIABILITIES

Current liabilities (debt due within
next 12 months)
   Bank loans                                _____
   Loans – other                             _____
   Accounts payable                          _____
   Current portion of long-term debt         _____
   Other current liabilities                 _____
Total current liabilities               (D)  _____

Long-term debt (less current portion)
   Mortgages                                 _____
   Loans from partners or stockholders (owner's equity)  _____
   Other loans of long-term nature           _____
Total long-term debt                    (E)  _____
Total liabilities (D + E = F)           (F)  _____
Net worth (C – F = G)                   (G)  _____
Total net worth and liabilities (F + G = H)  (H)  _____
```

Figure 17.8. *New client record sheet*

	File No. _____
	Telephone no. _____
Name	_____
Address	_____
	_____
	_____

Lead
  Date of enquiry _____
  Person making enquiry _____
  Source of referral _____
  Nature of initial enquiry _____
  Consultant contacted _____
  Follow-up planned

Dates of:
  Phone conversations _____
  Meetings _____
  Correspondence _____
  Total time expended on client
  prior to any proposal
  preparation _____

Proposal
  Presentation date of proposal _____
  Time required to complete
    proposal _____
  Cost estimate _____
  Consultant with primary
    responsibility for
    assignment _____
  _____

Assignment
  Starting date _____
  Consultant(s) assigned _____
  Primary client contact _____
  Total billing _____
  Completion date _____

Figure 17.9. *Assignment record sheet*

ASSIGNMENT RECORD SHEET

CLIENT DETAILS
Name . . . .
Address . . . .
Telephone no. . . . .
Name of contact (and address and telephone number if different)

ASSIGNMENT DETAILS
Type of assignment . . . .
Consultant in charge . . . .
Other assigned consultants:

names	from	to	time (days/hours)

Date proposal made . . . . Date proposal accepted . . . .
Date started . . . . Date completed . . . .

FEES AND TIMES

	Fee rate	Estimated time	Actual time	Estimated fee £	Actual fee £	Actual expenses £
Consultant in charge Other consultants						

Total fees received (excluding VAT)   £ . . . .
VAT   £ . . . .
Total value of expenses received   £ . . . .

COMMENTS (including follow-up action)

Figure 17.10. *Assignment diary*

ASSIGNMENT DIARY						
Client						
Type of assignment						
Assignment responsibilities of consultant						

Diary for week ending . . . .

Date	Activity	Time spent	Progress			Expenses incurred (specified)
			Time budget	Time to date	Complete	

Signed (consultant) . . . . Date . . . .

Countersigned (consultant in charge) . . . . Date . . . .

Figure 17.11. *Assignment control sheet*

ASSIGNMENT CONTROL SHEET

Client.......................... Report for week ending..........................

Activity	Programme reference number	Consultant	Completion date	Time this week		Total time		Activity completed
				Budget	Actual	Budget	Time to end week	
								✓

Signed (consultant in charge)........................... Date..............

Figure 17.12. *Consultant's brief and budget*

CONSULTANT'S BRIEF AND BUDGET

Consultant

Client

Type of assignment

Starting date . . . . Completion date . . . .

Brief (overall task to be accomplished by consultant)

Activity	Programme reference number	Budgeted time per week number:												Total time
		1	2	3	4	5	6	7	8	9	10	11	12*	

*Use continuation sheet if necessary.

Figure 17.13. *Weekly time sheet*

WEEKLY TIME SHEET

Consultant................ Week commencing................ Signed................ Date................

	Chargeable time		Non-chargeable time*						Public holiday or annual holiday entitlement	Total time
	Client's name	Time charged	Survey	Preparing proposal	Practice development	Product development	Personal development	Sick	Other (specify below)	Total		
Monday												
Tuesday												
Wednesday												
Thursday												

Friday															Total non-chargeable time – excluding public and annual holidays and non-chargeable time outside normal working hours	% of chargeable time
Saturday																
Sunday																
Total																
Grand total – chargeable time																

*Exclude time spent outside normal working time except weekends.

Figure 17.14. *Monthly summary time sheet*

		MONTHLY TIME SUMMARY – CHARGEABLE AND NON-CHARGEABLE TIME						Month ending	
Consultant	Chargeable time	Non-chargeable time*							
		Survey	Preparing proposal	Practice development	Product development	Personal development	Sick	Other	Total
Total									

*Excluding holidays and time outside normal working hours.

Chargeable time per cent	%

Figure 17.15. *Loading sheet*

Consultant	Week ending											
Total												

LOADING SHEET FOR 12 WEEKS ENDING . . . .

Chapter 18

Credit, Invoicing, and Collection

Many consultants starting out in businesses are more interested in performing their skilled service than developing a clear credit, invoicing and collection policy. In many cases a consultant has had no previous business experience and does not realise the pitfalls that can exist.

A rigidly followed system is essential to your survival. It does not take many bad debts to eliminate completely the profit of the business for the whole year. In more serious cases, you could go out of business if a substantial debt owing by a client is not paid.

A number of common mistakes are made by inexperienced consultants. First, the consultant, wanting to build up a clientele and reputation as quickly as possible, takes on many clients, performs the service and incurs expenses, but allows the client to defer payment. Second, the new consultant may be too busy or too inexperienced to monitor debtors carefully. Third, unpaid bills are not followed up quickly with appropriate steps to collect debts. The effect of this sloppy approach can be disastrous.

This chapter outlines the pitfalls to be aware of and the procedures to adopt when reviewing your debt collection policy. If you develop the correct system for your needs, it will enhance your cash flow and profit and minimise stress, client problems and bad debts.

Disadvantages of extending credit

When you extend credit, the understanding is that the client intends to pay, is capable of paying, and that nothing will occur to prevent the client from paying. You assume that most clients are honest and acting with goodwill and in good faith. Many of these assumptions may not be accurate.

There are a number of potential disadvantages to extending credit.

Extending credit may take a great deal of your time, and the administrative paperwork – checking references, monitoring and following up on slow-paying clients – may be tedious.

The expense of credit checking and collection could be more than you wish or are able to pay. Expenses could consist of credit reporting agency fees and memberships, collection costs, legal fees, and time lost that you could otherwise spend generating revenue.

You will need to increase your working capital requirements to keep your business in operation because receivables from your clients may or may not be paid when you expect or need them. You will be paying interest on the additional working capital that you may have to borrow to offset your decreased working capital.

Assessing the client

It is important to be very careful about extending credit. Apply the following general guidelines to your business.

(a) Develop a clear credit policy for your business after consultation with your accountant and your solicitor. Experienced professional advice is essential before you extend credit.

(b) Develop a credit application information sheet that has all the necessary information for your files.

(c) Consider joining a credit bureau as well as a credit reporting agency such as Dun and Bradstreet. Check into the past debt payment profile of your potential client in advance.

(d) Obtain references from your client if appropriate, and check the references. Ask about the client's length of time in business.

(e) Ask the client if consultants have been used before and the method of payment that was negotiated.

(f) Consider carefully the amount of credit being extended. The greater amount of money unpaid, the greater the risk for you.

(g) If the work you do is highly specialised, and you have very little competition, you have a lot of leverage in the nature of credit that you would be extending.

(h) If the client is a large institution or government, ask about the customary length of time for accounts rendered to be paid. Specify in your contract the exact terms of payment; government payments in particular can be delayed by bureaucracy for two or three months or longer.

(i) If the client requests deferred fees, you run a risk of default or other problems. Sometimes clients request a deferment of fees or payment because it is a large project, the client is suffering cash flow difficulties or other considerations. If you are faced

167

with a decision about deferral of fees, you should consider charging interest on the total amount, charging higher fees, requesting a sizeable retainer fee before you start the project, or obtaining collateral to protect yourself if your total fees are substantial.

(j) Consider the future benefit of a relationship with the prospective client. If there is a possibility of future contracts or sources of contacts with other prospective clients, you may wish to weigh the benefits against the risks.

Avoiding client misunderstandings on fees

Communication is vital to minimise client misunderstanding on fees. Many consultants feel uncomfortable discussing money matters during the first interview with the client; or sometimes consultants become so involved in the client's problem that the fee is not discussed. It is important that the amount of money you expect is understood and agreed upon by the client before you begin work.

Three ways to eliminate misunderstanding on the issue of services performed for fees are through communication, written contract and invoice.

Communication

Communication is a critical element in a satisfactory client relationship. The interview should be followed by a letter of confirmation. Progress reports should be sent to the client from time to time if the circumstances warrant it; copies of correspondence concerning the client should be sent to the client. If appropriate, try to involve the client with the project in some way so he or she feels a bonding to you in the project, and sees and appreciates the work you are doing on an ongoing basis. This should minimise the risk of a client disputing your fees for services.

Written contract

A written contract must be signed before work is begun. The contract can take various forms as outlined later in Chapter 20. Basically, a letter of agreement or formal contract explains the nature of fees involved and the method of payment – whether it is payment upon receipt, net 10 days or net 30 days.

Be very wary about financing a client; if at all possible, have payment upon receipt. This should assist your cash flow and minimise the risk of late payments. The contract should also state the interest that will be added to the outstanding debt if it is not paid within the terms of the contract. The contract should spell out in detail the exact services that you will be performing for the fee.

In certain circumstances a stop work clause could be inserted in the agreement to the effect that if payment is not made within the terms of the contract, at the option of the consultant, all work will stop.

Finally, the contract must be signed by the client decision-maker in authority. It is preferable that this individual is the same person with whom you negotiated the contract.

Invoice

To minimise misunderstanding on invoiced amounts, it is advisable to provide a detailed breakdown of the charges for services and expenses for the particular phase of the contract. If appropriate, reference should be made on the invoice to the contract agreement on fee structure and method of payment.

Minimising risk of bad debts

There are several effective techniques to minimise the risk of bad debts. As discussed previously, most consultants cannot afford to have one or two non-paying clients without seriously affecting the viability of the business. The following general guidelines may not all be appropriate in a given client situation. Your judgement in each case must dictate the appropriate approach.

Advance retainer

A client can be asked to pay a retainer or deposit of 10 to 25 per cent or more of the total contract amount prior to the work being carried out. This can be justified on the grounds that you are very busy, and if you are going to schedule in a commitment to that client, it is your policy to require an advance commitment retainer.

This is also an effective technique for a potentially high-risk client who has a reputation for non-payment or late payment, or who constantly argues about invoices. This approach can also be considered when dealing with a new client who has not used consultants before.

Pre-paid disbursements

Depending upon the length of the job and the type of client, you may wish to request pre-paid disbursements if the disbursements are going to be sizeable. You do not want to carry the client for out-of-pocket expenses at the risk of your own cash flow. You also do not want to run the risk of a non-payment or dispute of the overall account. As mentioned earlier, it is one thing to lose your time, it is another thing also to be out of pocket.

Progress payments

It is common for consultants to request funds by means of invoicing at specific points in the project. The stages at which progress payments are to be paid would be outlined in the contract.

Regular invoicing

Statements can be sent out on a weekly or monthly basis, depending on the circumstances. It is important to outline in the contract, if appropriate, your policy on the timing of invoices. That way the client will not be taken by surprise. This also provides you with the advantage of knowing at an early stage in the consulting project if the client is going to dispute your fees, and at this point you can either resolve the problem or discontinue your services. It can be very risky to allow substantial work to be performed before rendering an account, or waiting until the end of the project.

Invoicing on time

Generally a client's appreciation of the value of your services diminishes over time. This is a common problem. It is important, therefore, to send your invoice while the client can see the benefit of the service you have provided. Present your final invoice at the completion of the project.

Accelerated invoicing

If you sense that the client may have problems paying the invoice or other factors cause you concern, accelerate your normal invoicing pattern. You want to receive payment on your account before difficulties present themselves.

The risk of rendering an account that states 'net 30 days' is that the client is not legally overdue in payment to you until after 30 days. If you become aware of client financial problems, it is difficult to begin legal action for a garnishee order before the 30-day period has expired.

Holding up completion of important stage of project

If client problems occur, you may wish to stop providing your services and resources at a critical stage until the matter has been resolved to your satisfaction.

Personal guarantee of principals of a company

Depending on the project and client, you may want to have the principals behind a company sign a formal contract as personal guarantors.

Monitor payment trends of clients

Record and monitor the payment patterns of clients so you can watch for trends that may place your fees at risk.

Follow-up of late payments

If you see an invoice is more than a week or 10 days overdue, begin the various steps of your collection system immediately.

Figure 18.1. *General invoice*

Smith Jones & Associates

Consultants

20 High Street
Anytown, Anywhere
Tel no.:

Reference number: Tax point:

To: ABC Ltd
      10 London Road
      Anytown, Anywhere

Re: Computing System Analysis

PROJECT CONSULTANT: John Smith

For professional services provided between July 15 and July 30, 19...

Review, analysis and recommendations relating to
computing system:

	£
Total professional services 28 hours @ £75 per hour	2100.00
VAT @ 15% on above	315.00
Direct expenses:	
Photocopies, long distance telephone calls, and car mileage	102.20
	2517.20

VAT registration number: ......

Involving client in assignment

As mentioned previously, try to involve the client in some fashion during each step of the project. By making your client aware of your services, benefits, time and skill, you should minimise problems that could occur because of an unbonded or remote relationship.

Invoicing for services

Invoicing requires a system that is carefully designed and effective. It is important to have a third party review your invoicing procedures before you open your business. Constantly examine your invoicing procedures, especially during the first year, to make sure they are effective. This also gives you an opportunity to review your fee arrangements to make sure you are bringing in the appropriate cash flow for the time you are spending. As mentioned previously, it is important to monitor each client's file to see general trends in your invoicing patterns.

Proper records must be maintained that detail the time and expenses incurred so that the invoice can be prepared at the appropriate time. You should have an established procedure for regular invoicing so outstanding accounts are rendered on a regular basis, thereby minimising collection disputes or bad debts.

When rendering an invoice, make sure you send the account either directly to the appropriate person who has the authority to pay your account, or deliver the invoice personally to the client. Your style, the client and the circumstances will decide the most appropriate approach.

You may choose to send a general invoice to your client outlining briefly the services performed, the number of hours, the expenses and the total fee. A note on the invoice might say, 'Detailed particulars are available upon request.' See Figure 18.1 for a general invoice and Figure 18.2 for a detailed invoice.

Your invoice should be rendered on your consulting firm's stationery showing your name, address and telephone number. Always use stationery, not a blank piece of paper with your name typed on it. Prepare three copies of the bill. Send the original and a copy to your client and keep a copy for your files.

The wording on your invoice should include the following:

(a) The tax point (the date of the invoice);
(b) The name and address of the person invoiced;
(c) The phase of the project that has been completed;
(d) An outline of the services performed;
(e) The consultants or other resource personnel who performed the services;
(f) The date services were performed, and the total time worked;
(g) Total charges for services at the agreed fee rate;
(h) The VAT charge on fees;
(i) Expense column separated and listed underneath the services column and then totalled;
(j) Total of fees and direct expenses payable by client;

(k) The date charges are due and payable (if appropriate, make a reference to 'as per letter of agreement (or contract) dated (month/year)'.

Why clients pay late

If you have established appropriate precautionary measures and a credit and invoicing policy, you should have very few overdue accounts. Overdue accounts will occur in any practice, however, and understanding your options should minimise your problems in this area.

There are several common reasons why a client might be late in paying for consulting services. The client could be indifferent to your deadlines. Some clients have a sloppy attitude about paying accounts due and are accustomed to being pressured or reminded frequently before they finally meet their obligations.

Institutional or government payment procedures sometimes involve a two- or three-month wait for accounts to be paid. This type of information is easily available by asking the right questions before you begin. Your account may be lost in the maze and require personal attention.

A client may deliberately delay payment in order to save money at your expense. You save the client interest on working capital if he or she can use your money for free. This is why you should have an interest factor for overdue accounts built into your initial contract as well as showing on the statement. If the overdue interest is high enough, it should act as an incentive for the client to pay on time. If this is in the contract, the client cannot argue that there was no agreement on overdue interest. Rendering a statement with the interest factor noted on it is not in itself evidence of an agreement between the parties on the amount of interest on overdue accounts.

A client may prefer to give priority to other creditors, where pressure to pay is greater.

The client may not have the money. This does not necessarily mean that the client is going out of business, but is cash poor at the moment. The technique to handle this problem is discussed in the next section.

Collecting late payments without legal action

Because of the expense, time wasted, stress and uncertainty of legal action, it is preferable to collect as much as you can from clients yourself. Some steps that you may wish to consider are:

Figure 18.2. *Detailed invoice*

Smith Jones & Associates

Consultants
20 High Street
Anytown, Anywhere
Tel no.:

Tax point:
File reference:
Invoice number:
Terms: Net cash

To: Mary Roberts
Chief Executive
ABC Ltd
10 London Road
Anytown, Anywhere

Re: Computing System Analysis

PROJECT CONSULTANT: John Smith

		£	
Professional services:			
July 15	Attendance at South Branch site to review operations (4 hours)	300.00	
July 17	Meeting with Mr Roberts to discuss findings (3 hours)	225.00	
July 19	Attendance at South Branch site to analyse operations (5 hours)	375.00	
July 22	Preparation of report and recommendations (8 hours)	600.00	
July 26	Meeting with Mr Roberts to review recommendations (3 hours)	225.00	
July 30	Prepare final report of recommendations (5 hours)	375.00	
Total professional services (28 hours @ £75 per hour)			£2100.00
VAT @ 15% on above			£ 315.00
Direct expenses:			
Photocopies of 5 progress reports (400 pages @ 8p)		32.00	
Long-distance telephone call on 20 July to Mr Roberts		4.20	
Car mileage (200 miles @ 33p per mile)		66.00	
			£ 102.20

Figure 18.2. *(continued)*

	£
Total direct expenses:	102.20
TOTAL	2517.20
VAT registration number:	

(a) Send out a reminder invoice with a courteous comment that the invoice is 'overdue and that perhaps it was an oversight or the cheque is already in the post'.

(b) The alternative to the above is to telephone the accounts department or the client directly to ask when the payment can be expected. Ask courteously if there was possibly a misunderstanding, or if they need further information or clarification on any matter. Make sure that you note in the client file the date and time, the person you spoke to at the client's office, a summary of the conversation and when payment can be expected.

(c) If you have not received payment within a week of the preceding step, send a letter stating that the account is in arrears and that it is to be paid on the terms of the contract. The alternative is to telephone the client again and ask about the reason for the delay.

(d) Another technique is to ask when the cheque will be ready. Say that you will be round to pick it up or will arrange for a courier service to do so as soon as they telephone your office to advise that it is ready.

(e) If the client has still not paid, stopping work on the project is another option.

(f) If the client refuses to pay, legal steps may be required immediately depending upon the size of the invoice, the importance of the client, the reasons for non-payment and the costs of legal action. Alternatively, you may decide to compromise with a client and settle for a reduced payment.

(g) If the client is unable to pay because of cash flow problems or other financial difficulties, you have to assess your options. If the client is not disputing the invoice and wishes to have credit, there are basically three options:

● *Payment by instalment:* the client would agree upon definite dates for payment and would send you the amounts owing upon receipt of statements from you.

- *Post-dated cheques:* you would receive post-dated cheques from the client for the agreed period, and in the agreed amount.
- *Promissory note:* the client would sign a promissory note agreeing to the total amount of the debt and the date on which the debt would be paid. The note should be signed by the principals if the client is a company. Interest on the full amount of the debt should be built into the promissory note. It is negotiable whether or not interest is added on to the other two payment plans.

(h) You may wish to assign the debt to a collection agency for which you will be charged a fairly large proportion of the amount collected. This is better than writing the account off as a total loss. Different agencies have different styles of collection, and one agency may achieve better results with your bad debts than another. If your client pays you directly during the period of the contract with the collection agency, you are obliged to pay the commission to the collection agency. Collection agencies are listed in Yellow Pages.

(i) Your solicitor may act for you as a debt collector.

Legal steps if account remains unpaid

If it is apparent that the client has no intention of paying you, or is objecting to your invoice, or is unable to pay you, legal action must be considered as a last resort. It is critical that legal action be commenced as quickly as possible after it becomes apparent that you will not be paid by other arrangements. At this stage you are not interested in keeping the client for present or future business. You just want to salvage the best of a bad situation. Legal action can be taken through the County Court for smaller debts and the High Court for larger ones. But before going to court, remember the costs and the time involved. Bear in mind that even if you get a judgement in your favour you might not get the money from your debtor. Recovering debts by legal action is something that the small firm should only consider doing in very special circumstances.

Bad debts and taxes

Keep an accurate record of any bad debt accounts and the procedures you went through to attempt to collect. Generally, you will be allowed to deduct bad debts from your other income, but this is a matter that should be discussed with your accountant as the laws and circumstances can vary.

Chapter 19

Tax Considerations

Sole trader and partnership taxation

If you set up your practice as a sole trader or as a partnership you will be taxed as self-employed. Sole traders are taxed as if business income were their own earnings. In a partnership, each partner is jointly liable for income tax on the whole of the profits, but individual partners are assessed for tax on their share of taxable profits. The amount of tax paid will be affected by personal allowances, mortgage interest on the home, and so on. Liability for tax also depends on tax planning which can involve legitimate tax avoidance (minimising tax liabilities within the law and the Inland Revenue rules).

Things to do at the outset

As soon as you start work on your own account, you should tell your local Inspector of Taxes. The best way is to complete and send him form 41G. His address appears in the local telephone directory under 'Inland Revenue'.

If you have given up your previous employment, you should send your local Inspector of Taxes the form P45 given to you by your last employer when you left.

You should tell the local office of the Department of Social Security, who need to know for National Insurance contribution purposes. You should do this even if you are continuing to work for an employer as well as working partly for yourself.

You will need to obtain record books in order to keep proper accounts (see Chapter 17).

If you employ someone in the business, you may have to deduct income tax under the Pay As You Earn arrangements (see later in this chapter).

If your taxable turnover exceeds certain limits, you must be registered for Value Added Tax (VAT) (also dealt with later).

Accounting periods

The first accounting period of a new business can be any period that you choose with the advice of your accountant. The second period will generally be 12 months ending on a date which then becomes your usual 'year-end'. Your accounting period need not coincide with the normal tax year starting 5 April. There may be some advantages, if your business is seasonal, to fix your tax year accordingly. If, for example, your highest earnings occur in the last quarter of the year you might wish to start your year on 1 October so that you have plenty of scope for tax planning in the following nine months.

Previous year basis of taxation

Income tax is normally assessed for the year ending on 5 April. However, if in your consultancy business you make up yearly accounts to another date, the profits shown by your accounts are taxed as if they were profits for a year ending 5 April in the following tax year. This is known as assessing profits on a preceding year basis. There are special rules for taxing your profits in the first three and last three years of business (the commencement and cessation rules) which are considered below.

Whatever your accounting date, income tax and Class 4 National Insurance contributions (the latter are dealt with later in this chapter) are payable in two instalments, the first on 1 January in the tax year in which your profits are assessed and the second on the following 1 July. This rule positively encourages taxpayers to improve their cash flow by having an accounting date just after 5 April, which is why many businesses have a 30 April year-end.

Commencement provisions

For the first income tax year in which you start your consultancy business (that is, the tax year ending on 5 April following the start of trading) the assessment is based on the profits made in the period from commencement to 5 April. If, as often happens, the first accounts are made up to a later date, a proportion is taken.

For the next income tax year, the assessment is based on the profits of the first 12 months.

For the third income tax year, the assessment is based on the profits of the 12 months ending on the usual accounting date in the preceding income tax year. If no year fits this description, the assessment is based on the profits of the first 12 months' trading.

Example 1

You started up your consultancy on 6 October 1988 and decided to make up accounts annually to 5 October. The income tax profits for the year ending October 1989 are £4000, for the year ending 5 October 1990 are £28,000 and for the year ending 5 October 1991 are £36,000. The assessments are:

1988-89 (based on 6 months to 5 April 1989) 6/12 × 4000	£2,000
1989-90 (based on 12 months' trading)	£4,000
1990-91 (based on year ending 5 October 1989)	£4,000
1991-92 (based on year ending 5 October 1990)	£28,000
1992-93 (based on year ending 5 October 1991)	£36,000

As will be seen, the great advantage of this arrangement is that, if your profits are relatively low in your first year (because of start-up marketing costs and a limited amount of chargeable time in the early months), your tax bill in the first two full years of operation is related to this tax profit figure. Thus, although your profits in 1989-90 are £28,000 you only pay tax on £4000. And in 1989-91, when your profits are £36,000, you are still only paying tax on £4000.

It is because of these commencement provisions that accountants may advise their clients to maximise their legitimate tax deductible expenditure in their first year's trading and so reduce the profit levels used as the basis for tax payments in the next two years.

A taxpayer may choose to have the assessments for the second and third years (but not one only of those years) based upon the profits made in those years. Such a claim is normally beneficial if profits are lower in the second year of trading than in the first. It is to be hoped that by a combination of good business and good tax planning you are not placed in this position, but just in case, Example 2 shows how it works.

Example 2

You start up on 6 October 1988 and decide to make up your accounts annually to 5 October. The income tax profits for the year ending 5 October 1989 are £26,000, for the year ending 5 October 1990 are £19,000 and for the year ending 5 October 1991 are £32,000. Initially, the assessments for 1989-90 and 1990-91 are £26,000 each year, but on application by the taxpayer (within seven years of the end of the second year of assessment) the assessments can be amended to:

1989-90 (based on year ending 5 April 1990)		
half of profits of year ending 5 October 1989	=	£13,000
plus half of profits of year ending 5 October 1990	=	£ 8,500
		£21,500

1990-91 (based on year ending 5 April 1991)

half of profits of year ending 5 October 1990	=	£ 8,500
plus half of profits of year ending 5 October 1991	=	£16,000
		£24,500

The assessment for 1991-92 is still based on the profits of the year ending 5 October 1990, so in this case the 1991-92 assessment is £19,000.

The assessment for 1992-93, based on the profits of the year ending 5 October 1991, is £32,000, on the same principle as in Example 1.

Cessation provisions

If you decide to wind up your consultancy, the assessment for the income tax year in which it ceases is based upon the actual income tax profits of the period from 6 April before the cessation to the date of cessation. The Inland Revenue has the power to revise the assessment for the two income tax years before the income tax year in which cessation occurs to amounts based on the actual income tax profits of those years.

Example 3

You cease trading on 5 July 1989 having regularly been making up accounts to 5 October. The profits have been as follows:

12 months to 5 October 1986	£22,000
12 months to 5 October 1987	£26,000
12 months to 5 October 1988	£20,000
9 months to 5 July 1989	£ 9,000

The assessment for 1989-90 will be based on the profits of the three months from 6 April 1989 to 5 July 1989, ie $3/9 \times 9000 = £3000$.

Initially the assessment for the two previous years will have been:

1987-88 (based on year to 5 October 1986)	£22,000
1988-89 (based on year to 5 October 1987)	£26,000
	£48,000

The Inspector will revise the assessments as follows to the actual profits of these two years because they exceed the amounts which have been assessed:

1987-88

6 months to 5 October 1987 $6/12 \times 26,000$	=	£13,000
6 months to 5 April 1988 $6/12 \times 20,000$	=	£10,000
		£23,000

1988-89
6 months to 5 October 1988 6/12 × 20,000   = £10,000
6 months to 5 April 1989 6/9 × 9000   = £ 6,000

£16,000

£39,000

You should obtain the advice of your accountant on the tax implications of ceasing to trade as these can create complications.

Trading expenses prior to setting up the business

If you are a sole trader or partnership setting up business, you are entitled to count as part of your trading expenses any relevant money you spent up to three years before you actually started trading. As a budding consultant you may have spent money on getting your brochure and stationery printed before launching your new career. These costs can be offset against the income that you eventually generate when you start trading. If you do make an income tax loss you can carry it forward against the future income from your consultancy. If you have other income in the same year as you make the loss, you can set the loss off immediately against that income. Furthermore, if you make an income tax loss in the first four years of trading it can be carried back and set off against your other income in the three years prior to the loss. But you cannot set a capital loss against income.

Income tax profit computation

The two most important rules for arriving at the profits of your business for income tax purposes are:

1. Capital expenditure is not an allowable deduction.
2. The only expenses which are deductible are those incurred wholly and exclusively for the purpose of the business.

These rules are discussed more fully below.

Capital expenditure

For income tax purposes a distinction is drawn between 'capital' expenditure and 'revenue' expenditure. In very broad terms, expenditure is capital when the value is not used up in the course of the year, and it is revenue when it recurs regularly year by year. Examples of capital expenditure are the cost of purchasing equipment, such as computers/word processors or fax machines, or the cost of purchasing a vehicle.

Although the cost of business equipment and vehicles cannot be claimed as a deduction in arriving at the amount of the profits, there are special allowances for the expenditure. These reduce the income on which tax is chargeable. You should seek advice from your accountant on the scope for claiming capital allowances.

When a car is used for both business and private purposes, a suitable division of capital allowances and running expenses has to be made. The tax inspector will need information about business and total mileage so that the division can be properly calculated. Journeys to and from a regular place of work are regarded as being for private, not business purposes.

Business expenditure

The rules for business expenditure are as follows:

(a) only business expenses can be deducted from income to calculate taxable profits;

(b) private or domestic expenses on items such as food, clothing and medical treatment are not allowable;

(c) other expenses which are not allowable include premiums on personal insurance policies, income tax, any salary paid to yourself and your own National Insurance contributions, and the costs of business entertaining;

(d) expenses which are allowable include accountancy fees, advertising, bad debts, employees' salaries, hire purchase charges, incidental costs of raising loan finance, insurance premiums for the business, interest paid on loans for the business, National Insurance contributions by employers, pension contributions for employers and employees, repairs, travelling expenses incurred wholly in connection with the business, this includes vehicle costs attributable to the business;

(e) heating, lighting, rates and telephone costs are allowable in full if they are wholly incurred in running the business. If, however, you are working from home, you will only be able to claim a proportion of the expenses;

(f) if you employ your wife or husband in the business the salary paid is an allowable expense, provided that the amount is appropriate and reasonable. PAYE has to be deducted and National Insurance contributions paid in these circumstances.

Value Added Tax

You must register with Customs and Excise for VAT if the value of your output is likely to exceed certain limits. From 15 March 1988 these limits were £22,000 per annum or £7500 per quarter. You should start charging your clients VAT and keep VAT records as soon as you know you are required to register. The 'VAT Pack' supplied by your local VAT office contains all the information you need about registration and administrative procedures. The following is a summary of the main points to be considered.

To register or not to register?

You have no choice but to register if your outputs are or are likely to be above the limit. You can register if you are below the limit but it does require a lot of paperwork and Customs and Excise have the right to refuse to register you. Some consultants register as a matter of course to demonstrate to their clients that they are in business in a reasonably big way. If in doubt, seek your accountant's advice.

The VAT system

Once registered, you must charge VAT at the current rate of 15 per cent on all the fees for your consultancy services. Your invoices must show your VAT registration number and full details of your charges, separating your fees from the VAT charge. There are simplified requirements for invoices under £50, but you are not likely to be invoicing amounts below £50 frequently, if at all, so these arrangements will not concern you.

You will, of course, be paying VAT yourself on business purchases and you must keep all the invoices you receive on which VAT has been charged and list them in a day book.

At the end of each VAT accounting period (usually quarterly) you must complete a VAT return of all your outputs showing their total value and the amount of VAT charged. Against this, you can set off the total value of your inputs (VAT on your purchases). If the value of your outputs (the amount of VAT paid to you) exceeds the value of your inputs (the VAT you have paid on your business purchases), you must pay the balance to Customs and Excise. If, on the other hand, you have paid more VAT on legitimate business expenses than you have received, you can claim the difference from Customs and Excise.

You must keep adequate VAT records, including the relevant documents. They will have to be produced if a VAT officer carries out an inspection. Customs and Excise have the power to keep records and documents for a maximum of six years from the end of your accounting period.

If in any doubt about VAT consult your accountant or your local VAT office.

National Insurance contributions

Self-employed individuals, including active partners, normally have to pay Class 2 contributions, and also Class 4 contributions on profits between certain limits.

Class 2 contributions are paid at a flat weekly rate (£4.05 in 1988-89). If annual earnings are expected to be below £2250 (1988-89), it is possible to claim exemption from this liability. These contributions are collected by the Department of Social Security, either by direct debit or by stamps on a card.

Class 4 contributions are paid by the self-employed in addition to Class 2 contributions on trading profits between, in 1988-89, a lower limit of £4750 and an upper limit of £15,860. The rate in 1988-89 was 6.3 per cent. Class 4 contributions are normally calculated, assessed and collected by the Inland Revenue at the same time as income tax on the business profits. In computing your total income you can deduct one half of the finally settled amount of Class 4 contributions you are liable to pay for that year of assessment.

Employees

If you have any employees you will have to operate the Pay As You Earn system and also pay National Insurance contributions. For further information consult 'The Employer's Guide to PAYE' available from HM Inspector of Taxes and 'The Employer's Guide to National Insurance Contributions', obtainable from the Department of Social Security.

Chapter 20

Consultancy Contracts

As a consultant, you will quickly become aware of the necessity of written contracts in all your business and client relationships. A contract is the framework within which your obligations, rights, remedies and remunerations are clarified. There are oral, written and implied contracts. You want to make sure that your consulting business assumes no commitments or financial outlay without the security of an agreement in writing. Many consultants and other small business people begin their business with the trusting attitude that a verbal agreement is sufficient. It only takes one bad experience to demonstrate the folly of relying on a verbal agreement. This chapter explores some of the important aspects of contracts.

Essentials of a valid contract

A contract is an agreement between two parties to perform mutual obligations. It is an agreement which is enforceable in law. An essential feature of a contract is an exchange of promises, express or implied, by the parties to do or forbear from doing certain specified acts. The most common forms of contract are the oral contract and the written contract. The problem with an oral contract is that if the parties disagree, unless there are reliable witnesses or part performance of the agreement, it is difficult to reconstruct what the original bargain was. A written contract simply records in a formal or informal manner the nature of the bargain. For example, if you send a letter to a client confirming your agreement and the five essential elements of a contract are present, you have a simple informal contract.

The five elements of a contract are as follows:

Offer

If you are submitting a proposal or a contract to a client, that constitutes your offer to the client to accept your proposal. Your offer, naturally, will be in writing and spell out the particulars in some detail.

Acceptance

Acceptance of your proposal must be clearly demonstrated. Normally, this takes the form of your prospective client confirming in writing an acceptance of your proposal letter or document or contract, and acknowledging the terms you have outlined.

In certain situations an acceptance can be assumed and the contract made valid by part performance. In other words, it could be argued that your offer was accepted if your client permitted you to perform in part or in full the terms of your written proposal, even though a written acceptance had not been received. Naturally, this is a high-risk manner of doing business. Never begin a project without first protecting yourself in writing.

Consideration

Consideration is something of value being promised to you or given to you in exchange for your services. Valuable consideration normally refers to money or some other valuable assets, but a promise to pay money or provide some other benefit can be deemed to be consideration.

Competency

An agreement will not be considered binding if signed by persons lacking competence to understand the 'nature and quality of their actions'. This includes minors, the mentally infirm, or a person who is intoxicated at the time the agreement was accepted or signed. The age at which a person ceases to become a minor varies depending upon the jurisdiction. In some circumstances a contract signed by a minor is considered to be binding.

Legality

A contract created to perform an illegal act is void. For example, if a number of businesses signed an agreement to price fix in their area of product sales, and one of the parties failed to follow the agreement, the other parties to the agreement would not be able to sue for breach of contract, as the subject matter of the agreement was illegal.

Why a written contract is needed

There are many reasons why a written contract is essential. Some of the reasons are:

- *Projects professional image.* A written contract enhances your image as a responsible professional and businessperson.
- *Avoids misunderstandings.* It is difficult to remember complex details

without having them in writing. Subsequent events and distractions can cloud the recall of earlier conversations. Both parties can have different assumptions and interpretations of what the bargain was on critical points of issue. It makes sense to prevent this problem by the simple act of writing down the agreement.

- *Untruthful client.* It is not uncommon in verbal agreements for one party to reconstruct the agreement in a self-serving fashion at some later point. This could be to negotiate a more favourable contract or to get out of the contract obligations all together. If it is just one person's word against the other, it is difficult (if not impossible) for a court to attempt to reconstruct with certainty the original bargain. The time, delay and expense of attempting to assert your rights eliminate any profit and possibly your business as well.

- *Death of either party.* If either party to the contract dies, the estate of the deceased would have difficulty determining the actual bargain. This could give rise to law suits against the estate of the deceased consultant if the client claimed damages had been suffered because of the death due to breach of contract. The estate of the deceased would be in a difficult position to defend any action, not knowing the exact terms and obligations of both parties.

- *Terms of payment outlined.* If you do not have specific terms of payment in writing, such as monthly or at specific stages in the project, the client could attempt to wait until the end of the job to pay you, claiming there was no other agreement to the contrary. You want to avoid this problem by having written agreement before you expend your time, energy and resources.

- *Fee for service confirmed.* You want to make clear that you are being paid for your time, and that your efforts are not being supplied free as a marketing device or preliminary assessment.

- *Avoiding and limiting liability.* You want to protect your interests in writing by having provisions in the agreement to protect yourself from liability. For example, you may want to have a contingency clause to the effect that if events occur outside your control you are not to be held responsible. You might also consider a limited liability clause which sets a fixed amount of money that you would be responsible for if you are held liable. For example, you might have a clause stating that your liability is limited to £10,000 or the balance of the contract, whichever is less.

- *Preventing litigation.* If you do not have an agreement in writing, a client could claim that you acted improperly or that the work was not completely done. Unless an agreement in writing spelled out the nature of the services that you were going to provide, it would be difficult for you or your client to show exactly what you agreed upon. Because of this impasse on the terms and obligations of the agreement, litigation might be difficult to avoid.

- *Collateral for financing.* A written contract outlining benefits that you will receive for performing services is as good as money. You can pledge the contract at a bank as security for loan advances. This ability to lever your legal documents for working capital or cash flow purposes is just good business sense. No banker will lend money on the strength of your verbal assurance that you have a consulting agreement with a client.

- *Potential for increase of revenue.* If you have a contract that details the exact services and supplies you are providing, any variation would allow you to negotiate an addendum to the agreement. The problem with an oral agreement could be a dispute over the exact point at which your services and supplies are not included in the bargain.

- *Independent contractor status confirmed.* Without a written agreement specifying your independent status of operating, within the terms of the agreement, without direction or control, you could be considered to be an employee by the tax authorities. Make clear in the written agreement the nature of the roles of the parties. Also, the client might set down his or her own specifications, or question you in detail on an ongoing basis about what you are doing, thereby reducing some of your independence. To prevent this, take the initiative and specify the detail, nature and form of the services you are going to provide.

- *Encourages contract acceptance.* Many prospective clients feel nervous about agreeing to have you perform a project unless they know the exact detail and terms of the relationship in writing. The person with whom you might be negotiating frequently has to explain the particulars to colleagues or superiors. Without a written contract, you might not win the assignment.

- *Communication.* As mentioned previously, good communication is an essential ingredient for client satisfaction and goodwill. A well-written contract helps build client confidence.

The basic consultancy contract

The basic consultancy contract consists of:

1. The written proposal, which describes the work you will do, how

you will do it, who will do it, the time scale (starting and finishing dates), fee scales, total cost estimate, if any, and the arrangements for paying your expenses.

2. Your standard terms and conditions which are attached to your proposal.

3. The client's acceptance in writing of your proposal and standard terms and conditions.

The standard terms and conditions should, as a minimum, contain clauses covering:

(a) the fact that these terms are related to a specified proposal;

(b) the arrangements for paying fees and expenses, including the timing of invoices (eg monthly) and the requirement for them to be settled on receipt;

(c) notice that fee rates may be increased as a result of inflation but that, in the event of an increase, three months' notice will be given;

(d) the basis upon which the consultant's time will be charged, ie a daily or hourly rate, charging for travelling time, not charging when the consultant is absent through illness or on holiday;

(e) the basis upon which expenses will be charged – listing the main headings;

(f) the arrangements for cancelling the assignment, eg two weeks' notice on either side, fees to be paid to the end of the period of notice.

Some terms and conditions statements include a clause to the effect that, while the time and cost estimates were given in good faith on the basis of the survey, circumstances might arise which could not have been foreseen at the time, necessitating an extension to the time required and therefore an increase in costs, to be agreed with the client. Some consultancies have much more elaborate formal contracts and the structure of such a contract is described below.

Structure of a formal contract

A consulting contract can vary widely in its complexity depending upon the nature and value of the project being performed and the nature of the clients being served. Figure 20.1 describes the format for a formal contract and discusses clauses that are frequently included. Not all the clauses are necessarily appropriate or applicable in each case. A simple contract or letter of understanding does not need the same detail.

If a proposal letter or document exists, it can be referred to in the contract as part of the agreement and attached as an appendix.

Figure 20.1. *Contract format*

---

1. **Parties involved:** Name all parties involved in the contract and state the date the contract is signed.

2. **Term of contract:** The starting and completion dates of the contract are written here, or a reference is made to an appendix attached in which the dates and hours are described. The contract may state either the beginning and ending dates of an assignment, or both, or a maximum of hours within a fixed time period. The time period can either be closed or open. An open contract simply states that a specific job is to be performed, without giving a deadline for completion; or a contract might simply state that an ongoing relationship is commencing, the length of which shall be at the pleasure of both parties.

3. **Duties of the consultant:** Outline your proposed consulting in detail, by specific task and scope. Previous meetings have probably clarified services to be offered during the proposal stage, and the proposal letter or document spells out what you are offering. If this is included in the contract for practical, tactical or legal reasons, or choice of style, the following areas might be covered:

- Services that you, as consultant, will provide;
- The timing of the submission of various documents pertaining to the project;
- The nature of reports to be furnished, if any, and the approximate dates when they will be completed;
- Any special materials to be prepared, such as brochures, etc;
- The timing and nature of any consultant/client meetings, either on fixed dates or at specific stages in the project or upon mutual request;
- Travel that might be required, the nature of compensation, when that is to be paid, and what is required to obtain payment;
- Your authority to use client resources, office equipment, computer, files and records, and access to client's customers;
- Your right to use third-party information; eg ledgers and journals and other financial information in the possession of the client;
- A provision restricting you from performing services for the client's competitors. (Be careful of this provision, especially if you intend to develop a clientele base within a certain industry.)

4. **Duties of the client:** Wherever a consultant requires access to information or to employees, customers or advisers of the client, it should be specified clearly in the agreement that the client agrees and will have the

---

responsibility of facilitating and performing in those specific areas. For example, if you require information from a third party, you should make the client responsible for obtaining the information for you. If the client does not or cannot cooperate and therefore impedes the project, how are you compensated?

5. **Payment for services:** This is an important section and should state the basis on which your fees will be paid; that is, per day, fixed rate, fixed price plus expenses or other form. (See Chapter 8.) When and how the invoices will be rendered should be spelled out clearly; eg invoices could be rendered at specific identifiable stages throughout the project. If the client is billing on an hourly or daily rate, it should be specified in the contract what that rate is. If a down payment (retainer) is required, that should also be specified.

6. **Expenses:** Any job-related expenses to be paid by the client are described here. In the case of a fixed price contract, your expenses are incorporated in the fixed price agreed upon. Most other forms of fee structure involve expenses to be paid by the client. Outline what is required for payment.

7. **Late payment:** The contract should specify when payment should take place – either at specified periods or upon receipt of invoice or 30 days after invoice, or whatever arrangement is agreed upon. A clause can be inserted in the agreement that if the invoice is not paid within the agreed invoicing period, interest on the overdue account will be added. The interest rate is normally slightly higher than the prevailing bank rate to act as an incentive to pay.

8. **Stop work clause:** This clause allows the consultant to cease providing services on the project until the outstanding fees and interest have been paid. Generally, this clause is not applied until a certain period has elapsed and all other attempts at getting payment through goodwill have been unsuccessful. Stopping work is a last resort. It is important that the basis on which you can discontinue your services is stated in the contract.

9. **Independent contractor:** State that you are an independent contractor and therefore not eligible to participate in any benefit programmes or tax withholding obligations on the part of the client. This clause makes it clear that you are not an employee.

10. **Work delegation:** Outline the basis on which you are permitted to hire assistants and delegate work. Depending upon the nature of services you are providing, your personal service and expertise is probably desired by the client. If you plan to subcontract out to other people, protect yourself by clarifying that in the contract.

11. **Additional work:** This clause allows a client to request a modification to the contract and add a provision for additional services. Any modification to the contract should be confirmed in writing with

particulars and signed by both parties before any additional service work begins.

12. **Confidentiality:** State that any information disclosed to you pertaining to the project or any information that you become aware of during the period of the project will be kept strictly confidential.

13. **Ownership:** This clause covers ownership of materials or ideas resulting from your services. Many rejected ideas and plans could be useful for another project. Naturally, it is not in your best interests to have the client own this information. You should require that rejected plans or ideas are to remain your property.

14. **Limited liability of consultant:** You may wish to insert a clause stating that any liability because of your mistakes or breach of contract is limited to the amount of the contract price, assuming that there is a fixed contract price, or the amount of loss, whichever is lower. If there is no fixed contract price, set a specific maximum to the loss. However, such a clause is difficult, if not impossible, to enforce. You should also consider taking out professional liability insurance and errors and omissions insurance as a protection. (See Chapter 22.)

15. **Contingencies:** This clause states that you have complete control of all services rendered, with the exception of events beyond the control of you or the client, such as accidents, delays, strikes or supplier problems. This clause attempts to protect both parties if the contract is not completed.

16. **Advertising:** This clause restricts the use of the client's name for media release without the written approval of the client.

17. **Arbitration:** Outline the procedures to be followed in the event of disagreement by either party about the terms or interpretation of the terms of the contract. Normally, provision is made for a dispute to be settled by an independent arbitrator, the basis on which the arbitrator will be paid and by whom, and the criteria for selecting the arbitrator.

18. **Governing laws:** This clause simply states that the contract shall be governed by the laws of the jurisdiction in which it is written.

19. **Termination:** Either party is allowed to terminate services upon written notification a set number of days in advance. Outline the details and the reasons under which termination can take place.

20. **Agreement binding:** State that the written agreement is the total agreement between the parties and shall take the place of any previous contracts or verbal or written agreements. This clause normally states that any modification to the agreement must be in writing and agreed between the parties to be enforceable.

21. **Signatures:** The parties to the contract sign the agreement. It is very important that a representative of the client who signs has the authority to do so and the position held is written on the contract. In some cases, company seals are required if companies are involved.

Types of contracts

There are several types of contracts frequently used in the consulting business. It is important to understand the options that are available to you as they involve various tactical and legal considerations. A brief summary of the most common types of contracts follows.

Letter of agreement

This simple contract is in the form of a letter stating a summary of the agreement between the parties. This includes the nature of services to be performed, the method and time of payment, the starting date and duration of the contract, the resource materials and personnel to be supplied by the client, if applicable, and the consultants who will be involved on the project, if applicable.

The letter of agreement is normally prepared by the consultant and forwarded to the client for signature and approval. An example of a letter of agreement prepared by a consultant is shown in Figure 20.2.

Figure 20.3 shows a letter of agreement prepared by the client. Note the differences in tone and format between the two. The one prepared by the client has the appearance of a short formal contract.

Letter of agreement with general terms and conditions appended

Another option is to have a letter of agreement accompanied by a statement of standard terms and conditions (see Figure 20.4). The statement is a standardised form that you can use often for similar types of agreements. It includes such matters as fee structure, reimbursable expenses, subcontracts, invoices and payments, warranty and limitation of professional liability. Other clauses can be included in this form based on your own needs and precautions. If you prefer this format, the letter of agreement attached to the terms and conditions need not be detailed. It can outline the specific, not general, terms of the agreement.

The letter of agreement and/or general terms and conditions form are frequently used if the client does not want a more formal contract. From a tactical viewpoint, you might feel that a client would be intimidated by a formally structured contract. Another factor might be your personal style of consulting practice. If the contract is not complex and the fee is low, you might favour the simpler contract format.

Formal contract

A formal contract is preferred if the financial cost of the project is high, if the project is complex, if substantial financial commitment to suppliers or subconsultants is involved, or if it is the style of the client to require such a detailed contract.

Normally, when government contracts are involved, the government prepares the formal contract.

Figure 20.2. *Letter of agreement*
(prepared by consultant)

(Consultant's letterhead)

_____ 19____

Mary Roberts, Chief Executive
ABC Ltd
10 London Road
Anytown, Anywhere

Dear Ms Roberts,

Re: Consulting Agreement

This letter will confirm our understanding concerning the terms of retainer and nature of services to be performed for ABC Ltd. These terms are as follows:

1. Term. This agreement will be for a period of _____ commencing on ___. Either of us may terminate this agreement with thirty (30) days' written notice to the other party. In the event of termination, I will be compensated for services rendered up to the date of termination.

2. Duties. My duties will include:

   (a) Review, analysis and recommendations for changes in the systems and organisational structure of the research division.

   (b) Preparation of weekly reports on the progress of the project.

   (c) Preparation of a final report and oral presentation for the management of the company, with recommendations for implementing system and organisational improvements and related costing.

3. Fee. The fee for my services shall be at the rate of £750 per day, payable on receipt as invoiced. Other out-of-pocket costs, such as travel expenses and secretarial services, will be invoiced separately at cost.

Enclosed is a copy of this agreement for your records. Please sign the original and return it to this office in the enclosed envelope. If you have any questions, please contact me.

Yours sincerely,

David Jones
Consultant

Accepted and agreed to:

_____   _____

Mary Roberts, Chief Executive   Date
ABC Ltd

Figure 20.3. *Letter of agreement*
(prepared by client)

ABC Ltd
10 London Road
Anytown, Anywhere

_____ 19 ____

Smith Jones & Associates
Consultants
20 High Street
Anytown, Anywhere

Dear _____,

Re: Consulting Project

I am pleased to announce that your proposal to ABC Ltd has been accepted. The conditions of our acceptance are as outlined below.

1. **Term.** Your appointment as a consultant to ABC Ltd (hereinafter called 'the Company') is confirmed for the period ____ to ____.

2. **Services.** You shall perform such work or services as are set forth in Exhibit A, attached hereto and specifically made a part of this Agreement. The work or services to be performed by you may be changed by the Company from time to time by letter requests sent to you. You

shall keep the Company informed on the progress of any work being performed under this Agreement.

3. **Fees and expenses.**

(a) The Company will pay you a total fee of £ _____ for all work performed hereunder on satisfactory completion of the work.

(b) Your fee will be at the rate of £ _____ per month for all work performed hereunder. You will be paid at the same time you are reimbursed for approved expenses under paragraph 3(c) below.

(c) You will receive reimbursement for the actual cost of reasonable expenses arising out of the work performed under this Agreement (not to exceed £ _____), subject to the approval of the Company. You shall deliver an itemised statement to the Company on a monthly basis that shows fully the work being performed under this Agreement and all related expenses. The Company will pay you the amount of any authorised expenses within thirty (30) days of the receipt of the itemised statement of all expenses, submitted together with receipts for all hotel, car rental, air fare and other transportation expenses for all other expenses of £20 or more.

4. **Working facilities.** You will be furnished with such facilities and services as shall be suitable for your position and adequate for the performance of your duties under this Agreement.

5. **Reports.** Any and all reports, manuscripts and any other work products, whether completed or not, that are prepared or developed by you as a part of the work under this Agreement shall be the property of the Company and shall be turned over to the Company promptly at the Company's request or at the termination of this Agreement, whichever is earlier.

6. **Independent contractor.** You shall exercise control over the means and manner in which you perform any work requested hereunder, and in all respects your relationship to the Company shall be that of an independent contractor serving as a consultant and not as an employee.

7. **Termination.** This Agreement may be terminated upon thirty (30) days' written notice by either party.

8. **Confidential information.** You agree that, for the term of your appointment hereunder and for two (2) years thereafter, you will not disclose to any person, firm or corporation any confidential information regarding the Company, its business, directors, officers and employees.

9. **Non-assignable.** This agreement is personal in nature and is not assignable by you or by the Company.

10. **Entire agreement.** This letter, including Exhibit A, contains the

entire agreement of the parties. It may not be changed orally but only by an agreement signed by the party against whom enforcement of any waiver, change, modification, extension or discharge is sought.

I trust that the terms of this appointment meet with your approval. If so, please indicate this by signing a copy of this letter and returning it to the Company. An additional copy of this letter is enclosed for your records.

Yours sincerely,

_____
Client signature

Accepted and agreed to this _____ day of _____ 19_____

_____
Consultant signature

Other situations where a formal contract might be considered are if you have a new client, a client who has never used consulting services before, or a client who has a reputation for being difficult in general, or complaining about fees in particular. Naturally, in this latter case, if you have advance notice it would be very wise to reconsider any involvement with that client.

Figure 20.5 illustrates a formal contract. Figure 20.6 is a checklist of provisions frequently covered in contracts.

Subconsulting agreement

This is an agreement between you and any subconsultants you employ to undertake a part or all of a consulting project you have arranged.

Figure 20.4. *Statement of general terms and conditions*

1. **Fee structure**

All time, including travel hours, spent on the project by professional personnel will be invoiced. The following approximate ranges of hourly rates for various categories of personnel are currently in effect.

Category	Hourly rate
Principal	£100
Consultant	£ 75

Hourly rates are liable to adjustment as necessary to reflect inflation. Three months' notice will be given before any such fee adjustment. Unless otherwise stated, any cost estimate presented in a proposal is for budgetary purposes only, and is not a fixed price. The budget figure will not be exceeded without prior authorisation from the client.

2. Reimbursable expenses
The following expenses will be invoiced at cost:

(a) Travel expenses necessary for the execution of the project, including air fares, rented vehicles and road mileage in company or personal vehicles, which will be charged at 32p per mile (this sum will be reviewed every six months). Air travel will be by club class, where available

(b) Telephone charges

(c) Postage

(d) Printing and reproduction

(e) Computer services, including word processing

(f) Other expenses directly attributable to the project.

3. Invoices and payments
Invoices will be submitted monthly and payment is due on receipt of invoice.

Rates for foreign contracts are negotiable and the above rates do not apply.

4. Warranty
Our professional services will be performed, our findings obtained and our recommendations prepared in accordance with generally and currently accepted management consulting principles and practices. The warranty is in lieu of all other warranties either expressed or implied.

5. Other documents
(eg Proposal letter dated _____) is hereby made a part of this document.

6. Acceptance by client
Client, by signing below, hereby agrees to these general terms and conditions of Client except as noted below:

CLIENT (typed name of client)

BY: _____

(Signature)
(Name and designation)

Figure 20.5. *Consulting contract*

ABC & Company (hereinafter called 'the Company') desires to use the expert assistance of _____ (hereinafter called 'the Consultant') in the field or fields in which the Consultant has professional qualifications.

1. Parties and relationships

The Company is engaged in the business of consulting and the provision of technical assistance and training to small business through the use of skilled independent contractors. The Consultant is a person who by education, training and experience is skilled in the provision of the service required.

2. Character and extent of services

(a) It is the mutual intent of the parties that the Consultant shall act strictly in a professional consulting capacity as an independent contractor for all purposes and in all situations and shall not be considered an employee of the Company.

(b) The Consultant reserves full control of his activities as to the manner and selection of methods with respect to rendering his professional consulting services to the Company.

(c) The Consultant agrees to perform his activities in accordance with the highest and best state of the art of his profession.

3. Period of service and termination

(a) The period of service by the Consultant under this agreement shall be from _____ to _____ and may be renewed upon the mutual agreement of the parties hereto.

(b) Either the Company or the Consultant may terminate this agreement by giving the other party thirty (30) days' written notice of intention of such action.

(c) The Company reserves the right to halt or terminate the conduct of a seminar/workshop by the Consultant without prior notice or claim for additional compensation should, in the opinion of the Company, such conduct not be in the best interests of the Company.

4. Fees

(a) Upon the Consultant's acceptance hereof, the Company agrees to pay the Consultant according to the following schedule:

(Insert fee rate or fixed fee and any allowance for or schedule of allowable expenses, if any.)

(b) In the event that the Company desires, and it is mutually agreed to by the Consultant, the Consultant's services may be used in the conduct of training/consulting programmes not specifically identified in paragraph 4(a). In such cases, the Company agrees to pay the Consultant on the basis of the following schedule:

(Insert fee rate or fixed fee and any allowance for or schedule of allowable expenses, if any.)

(c) In the event of special circumstances, variations to the fee schedule of paragraphs 4(a) and 4(b) will be allowed as mutually agreed to in writing by the parties hereto.

5. Notification

The Consultant will be notified by the Company in writing to begin his participation in specific training and/or consultation assignments to which the fee schedule of paragraphs 4(a) and 4(b) applies. Such notification will include a statement of the time(s) and place(s) of the intended training/consultation involvement with other necessary information.

6. Expenses

The Consultant, as an independent contractor, shall be responsible for any expenses incurred in the performance of this Agreement, except as otherwise agreed to in writing prior to such expenses being incurred. The Company will reimburse the Consultant for reasonable travel expenses incurred with respect hereto.

(A specification of 'reasonable' may be inserted here.)

7. Method of payment

(a) The Consultant shall be paid as provided for in paragraphs 4(a) and 4(b) hereof, on the basis of a properly executed 'Claim for Consulting Service' form (sample attached).

(b) The 'Claim for Consulting Service' form is to be submitted at the end of the calendar month during which consulting services are performed. Exceptions to this arrangement are allowed with the written approval of the Company.

(c) Payment to the Consultant will be made by cheque, despatched not later than _____ days subsequent to receipt of the 'Claim for Consulting Service' form as provided for in paragraphs 7(a) and 7(b).

8. Copyrights

(a) The Consultant agrees that the Company shall determine the disposition of the title to and the rights under any copyright secured by the Consultant or his employee on copyrightable material first produced or composed and delivered to the Company under this agreement. The Consultant hereby grants to the Company a royalty fee, non-exclusive, irrevocable licence to reproduce, translate, publish, use and dispose of, and to authorise others to do so, all copyrighted or copyrightable work not first produced or composed by the Consultant in the performance of this Agreement but which is incorporated into the material furnished under this Agreement, provided that such licence shall be only to the extent the Consultant now has or prior to the completion or final settlement of this Agreement may acquire the right to grant such licence without becoming liable to pay compensation to others solely because of such grant.

(b) The Consultant agrees that he will not knowingly include any copyrighted material in any written or copyrightable material furnished or delivered under this Agreement without a licence as provided in paragraph 8(a) hereof or without the consent of the copyright owner, unless specific written approval of the Company to the inclusion of such copyrighted material is secured.

(c) The Consultant agrees to report in writing to the Company promptly and in reasonable detail any notice or claim of copyright infringement received by the Consultant with respect to any material delivered under this Agreement.

9. Drawings, designs, specifications

(a) All drawings, sketches, designs, design data, specifications, notebooks, technical and scientific data, and all photographs, negatives, reports, findings, recommendations, data and memoranda of every description relating thereto, as well as all copies of the foregoing, relating to the work performed under this Agreement or any part thereof, shall be subject to the inspection of the Company at all reasonable times; and the Consultant and his employees shall afford the Company proper facilities for such inspection; and further shall be the property of the Company and may be used by the Company for any purpose whatsoever without any claim on the part of the Consultant and his employees for additional compensation, and subject to the right of the Consultant to retain a copy of said material shall be delivered to the Company or otherwise disposed of by the Consultant, either as the Company may from time to time direct during the progress of the work, or in any event, as the Company shall direct upon the completion or termination of this Agreement.

10. Confidentiality

(a) It is understood that in the performance of his duties, the Consultant will obtain information about both the Company and the Company's client, and that such information may include financial data, client lists, methods of operating, policy statements and other confidential data.

(b) The Consultant agrees to restrict his use of such above-mentioned information to the performance of duties described in this Agreement.

The Consultant further agrees to return to the Company and to the Company's client upon the completion of his duties any and all documents (originals and copies) taken from either organisation to facilitate the project described herein.

11. Non-competition

The Consultant agrees that he will not perform his professional services for any organisation known to the Consultant to be a client of the Company unless the Company has employed the Consultant for the provision of such services to the client. This restriction shall remain in effect for a period of two years after the termination of this agreement. For the purposes of this section, 'client' is defined as any organisation which, during the said period of restriction, has engaged the Company to promote:

(Provide a list of all the services/products provided by the Company.)

12. Assignment

The Company reserves the right to assign all or any part of its interest in and to this Agreement. The Consultant may not assign or transfer this Agreement, any interest therein or claim thereunder without the written approval of the Company.

13. Integration

This Agreement, executed in duplicate, constitutes the entire contract between the parties and may be cancelled, modified or amended only by a written supplementary document executed by each of the parties hereto.

IN WITNESS WHEREOF, the parties hereto have accepted and executed this Agreement this _____ day of _____ 19 ____.

_____   _____
John Smith, Consultant   ABC & Company

                                by: _____
                                (Authorised signatory)

Figure 20.6. *Detailed contract checklist*

General

1. Date of agreement.

2. Identification of client and consultant, including transfer of responsibility to successors (if the client is a public body, the authority under which it acts and the source of available funds should be specified).

3. Review of the background and brief definition of the project.

4. Scope of the assignment, including references to any detailed description incorporated in appendices.

5. Effective date of commencement of work, when different from 1., and estimated or stipulated time for completion.

6. Designation of individuals in client and consultant organisations responsible for policy decisions.

7. Work statement containing a description of the requirements in detail. (The description should include the problem to be solved or the objective of the investigation, the approach or method to be used, and the extent or degree of work to be undertaken. The proposed statement of work should be sufficiently descriptive so as to become a usable yardstick.)

8. Provision for changes in the work requirements.

9. Provision for arbitration of disputes.

10. Provision for termination by either party for 'cause' or 'convenience'.

Responsibilities of the consultant

1. Specify a project leader, professional help, services and information to be supplied.

2. Work schedule to be maintained.

3. Personnel to be supplied (may be detailed in appendix).

4. Availability for conferences with the client.

5. Reporting, including the schedule and nature of reports.

6. Ownership of designs, blueprints, reports etc, to be specified in the contract.

7. Safeguarding of information supplied by client.

8. Guarantee of performance, where required.

9. Limitation of liability of the consultant with regard to loss or damage of reports, third-party use of reports, errors or omissions or professional negligence (this provision for the benefit of the consultant).

10. Right to cancel the contract upon written notice of (x) days, provided that non-performance of the other party can be clearly documented and provided that the defaulting party has been given (x) days to make good non-performance.

11. Provision for disposal of any or all materials used in the performance of work.

Responsibilities of the client

1. Information, services and facilities to be provided.

2. Availability for conference with the consultant.

3. Number of days of staff support by client agency staff.

4. Prompt review and approval of reports and products.

5. Changes clause.

Duration of contract

1. Stipulation of termination, either by stating a specific date, or by indicating the duration of the operation from the execution of the contract.

2. Provision and mechanism for the modification of the specified date by mutual agreement.

3. Provision for extension or renewal.

4. Provision and mechanism for early termination by either party.

5. Termination by reason of events beyond control of either party.

6. Provision against delays.

Financial provisions

1. Total financial commitment by the client.

2. Method and schedule of invoicing by the consultant.

3. Method of payment.

4. Currency or currencies of payment and conversion rates.

5. Guarantee of payment by the client.

6. Payment of interest on delayed payments.

7. What are patent requirements? Who has copyright in reports and other products? Who has publication rights and under what circumstances?

8. Payment shall be made within (x) days of invoicing, invoicing to be by arrangement.

9. Allowable costs or expenses to be invoiced separately from labour costs shall include but not be limited to:

> Telephone
> Postage and courier
> Travel
> Accommodation and miscellaneous
> Photocopying and printing
> Graphics
> Special typing support
> Translation
> Miscellaneous special materials
> Computer costs
> Subcontractual services
> Word processing
> Fax costs.

It is quite common for consultants to subcontract work out to other consultants. You may use subconsultants to keep overheads low, or if you are unable to perform the task yourself because you lack expertise in the area, or because a large project requires a large number of support resource personnel.

Generally, you need not explain to your client that you are using subcontracting services, unless your client specifically asks. Sometimes a client would like to have the qualifications of a subcontractor clarified. You are ultimately responsible for the quality of the work performed by your subconsultants and therefore must be very selective. You should monitor and approve all work performed by the subconsultant. All services performed by the subconsultant are performed under your consulting company's name. All correspondence pertaining to the project is printed only on your stationery. In all outward respects, the subconsultant is your employee under direction.

Your subcontracting agreement should clearly spell out that the relationship of the subconsultant to you is one of an independent contractor. You should also seriously consider a non-competition clause in the contract restricting the subcontractor from taking advantage of access to your clients to sell consulting services directly. A non-competition clause or restrictive covenant can vary depending upon the circumstances and the laws of your jurisdiction. Legal advice should be obtained before you complete any contract to be certain that the non-competition clause would be reasonably upheld as fair and appropriate if it were contested. The clause normally states that the subconsultant shall not perform professional services independently of your firm to any of your clients past or present. The exception would be under your direct employ as an independent contractor. A two-year time period for the restriction is fairly common. The restriction covers a wide or narrow geographic base depending on the nature of your services.

A summary of the standard clauses that should be considered include:

(a) The parties to the contract;
(b) Independent contractor status of subconsultant;
(c) The responsibilities of the subconsultant fully specified;
(d) Term of the contract;
(e) Amount and method of payment for fees and expenses;
(f) A cancellation provision in case the contract is cancelled;
(g) The method and amount of remuneration to be paid to the subconsultant up to the point of cancellation;
(h) A confidentiality provision stating that all the client information accessible to the subconsultant is to be held in strict confidence;

(i) All documents obtained by the subconsultant are to be returned to the consultant or client;

(j) Provision that the contract cannot be assigned or duties delegated without the written consent of both parties;

(k) Other 'standard' or 'unique' provisions.

Figure 20.5 which shows a consultant contract can also be used as a format for a subconsulting contract.

Agency agreement

An agency agreement is a contract that would be prepared if you were acting for a client as an external agent; for example, if you were selling a product on behalf of a client, or negotiating on behalf of the client with the government for funding purposes. The clauses in this type of contract vary considerably. Generally, the client prepares the agreement for you to sign.

Letter of retainer agreement

This is an agreement that you outline in a letter. One form of retainer relationship is when you are available 'on call' at the request of a client based on need of your services. The consultant charges the client for being 'on call' and available, even though the consultant may not be used.

Another form of retainer relationship is if you provide a service on a periodic basis, for example, monthly or quarterly.

Preparing your own contract

You should consider having several standard contracts with variations depending on the different types of consulting services you perform. Space can be left in the contract for inserting the unique features of a specific consulting project. If your contracts are stored on a word processor or a personal computer with word processing capabilities, each contract can easily be personalised in an original format for each consulting job.

The process of preparing your own contract is not difficult. Try to obtain as many samples of contracts as possible from your competitors. Then refer to the various headings outlined in this chapter or shown in the sample contracts or checklists. Outline the areas that you feel are important for your particular type of consulting services or problems. As soon as you have completed this exercise, expand on the points in a descriptive paragraph and then subdivide into clauses in a format appropriate to your needs and in a style you prefer.

Take your draft contracts to your legal adviser to evaluate. It is to your benefit to save your solicitor's time and your money by preparing the documents yourself. You are most familiar with your work and the important factors of your projects. Your solicitor can review your draft contracts and rewrite them or add additional clauses if required.

Major companies or government departments frequently have their own standard contracts and send them to you for signature. In some cases there is room for negotiation; in other cases no negotiation is possible. If you are presented with the contract, you should review it thoroughly yourself and mark the areas that cause you concern. Also, note the areas not in the contract that you would prefer to have covered. Then discuss the contract with your solicitor. If you have any doubts about the required provisions of the contract, it is best either to negotiate those provisions out if possible, or not accept the project. If a contract is not completely to your liking, the degree of risk or dissatisfaction on your part or your client's part is high.

If a client wants to make changes to your contract, it is better to make the changes rather than have them make up their own contract. A client-prepared contract could have clauses or conditions you do not want.

In summary, try to prepare all your own contracts. The client relationship will therefore be established on *your* terms. Your initiative and leadership in preparing the contract should have a positive effect on the dynamics of the relationship with your client.

Chapter 21

Insurance and Pensions

Insurance

Proper risk management means planning for potential problems and attempting to insure against them. You should be familiar with the numerous types of insurance available, the method of obtaining the insurance, the best way to reduce premiums and the pitfalls to avoid.

Obtaining insurance

Insurance companies market their services chiefly through the methods discussed below.

Agencies

These are normally the smaller individualised operations that place home, car or other common types of insurance with several insurance companies to which they are contracted. In some cases, small agencies, to earn their commission, are under an obligation to place a certain volume of insurance with each company they deal with. Therefore, it is possible that you might be sold policies offered by companies which may not suit your needs and may not necessarily be placed on a competitive basis.

Insurance brokers

Insurance brokers claim to have complete independence from any insurance company and more flexibility than the common agencies. In comparison with agencies in general, brokers from the larger companies are more knowledgeable and flexible in the types of coverage and policies available, and they specialise in certain areas. Also, a broker should have no vested interest in placing insurance with any particular company, and will therefore attempt to get you the best price and the best coverage to meet your needs. You should make specific enquiries to satisfy yourself.

As in all matters of obtaining professional advice or assistance, you should have a minimum of three competitive quotes and an opportunity to evaluate the relative strengths and weaknesses of each. If the brokers are using the same insurance base for the best coverage and premiums, all three brokers should recommend to you, in theory, the same insurance companies for the different forms of coverage you are requesting.

Planning your insurance portfolio

It is important to consider all criteria to determine the best type of insurance for you and your business. Your major goal should be adequate coverage, avoiding both over- and under-insurance. This is done by periodic review of risk, and by keeping your agent informed of any changes in your business that could potentially affect your coverage.

The following principles will help in planning an insurance portfolio:

(a) Identify the risk to which your business is exposed.

(b) Cover your largest risk first.

(c) Determine the magnitude of loss the business can bear without financial difficulty, and use your premium expenditure where the protection need is greatest.

(d) Decide what kind of protection will work best for each risk:
- Absorbing risks
- Minimising risks
- Insuring against risks with commercial insurance.

(e) Insure the correct risk.

(f) Use every means possible to reduce costs of insurance:
- Negotiate for lower premiums if loss experience is low
- Use excesses where applicable
- Shop around for comparable rates and analyse insurance terms and provisions offered by different insurance companies.

(g) Risk exposure changes, so a periodic review will save you from insuring matters that are no longer exposed to the same degree of risk. Conversely, you may need to increase limits of liability. Reviews can help to avoid overlaps and gaps in coverage, and thereby keep your risk and premiums lower.

(h) If you are pleased with a particular broker who can handle your various forms of insurance, it is preferable to be selective and have just one firm. An advantage of the larger broker firms is that they have a pool of insurance professionals expert in various areas as resource people for you.

(i) Attempt to keep your losses down in every way. Although your business may have adequate coverage, losses could be uninsurable, exempt from coverage, or have a large excess. Problems with insurance coverage could seriously affect the survival of your business.

Types of insurance

The main types of insurance you will have to consider are:

- Office insurance – loss or damage to office contents, legal liabilities, loss of revenue, bad debt cover, computer damage etc;
- Jury service – cover can be provided against the financial loss sustained by a consultant if he or she is involved in lengthy jury service;
- Personal accident or sickness – cover against accidental death, permanent total disablement and temporary total disablement;
- Business travel – package policies can be obtained on a worldwide basis providing cover in respect of business travel (including incidental holidays) covering medical expenses, baggage, money, personal accident, cancellation or curtailment, personal liability and hijack risks;
- Motor insurance;
- Life insurance;
- Employer's liability – personal injury or damage to personal property of employees;
- Professional liability – dealt with in Chapter 22.

Pensions

If you are practising on your own as an independent consultant you will need to take out a personal pension. Investing in a pension scheme is not just a method of providing income when you eventually retire, it is also probably the most tax-beneficial saving and investment vehicle available to you. The main benefits are:

1. Tax relief is given on your contributions at your top rate of tax on earned income.
2. Pension funds are in themselves tax exempt. Thus your capital builds up considerably more quickly than it would do in stocks and shares.
3. When you take your benefits you can have part of them as a regular pension payment and part as a lump sum of up to £150,000, which will not be liable to capital gains tax.
4. Lump sum benefits arising in the event of your death are paid out to your dependants free of inheritance tax.

5. Your pension is portable, ie it remains your personal property even if you cease to be a sole trader and join a firm with a pension scheme.

The only restriction placed on you by the government is that the amount you can contribute to your personal pension is limited to 17.5 per cent of your income. If, however, you were born between 1916 and 1933 you may contribute 20 per cent of your relevant earnings.

There are a lot of personal pension plans on offer and their virtues will be extolled vigorously by the pension firm sales staff. It is best to seek advice on the choice of a scheme from a registered pensions broker.

If you are setting up a firm with a number of partners and/or employees you will have to consider introducing a company pension plan. If the firm has 12 or fewer employees this can take the form of a small self-administered pension scheme (SSAS). The choice between a company scheme and personal pensions is highly complex and you should seek the advice of your broker on the best approach for your firm.

Chapter 22

Professional Liability

Consultants have the same degree of potential for law suits against them as do other professionals, such as doctors, accountants and solicitors. The claims made against the consultant could be that the consultant was responsible for a wrongful act or omission or professional misjudgement. Professional liability claims may be brought by the client or by third parties, such as investors, creditors or lenders.

If the consultant is doing business as a proprietorship or partnership, liability extends to the consultant personally. It may even extend to the consultant's estate after death. Liability can also extend to people who were the consultant's partners at the time of the alleged negligence. Claims may be made by the client long after the error or omission occurred. The statute of limitations in many instances will not begin until the claimant discovers or should have discovered, or knows or has reason to know of your alleged mistake.

As a consultant, you must weigh the degree of risk involved in your specific area of practice. Obtain expert legal and insurance advice about the proper methods of protecting yourself.

Contract and tort liability

It is not uncommon for a consultant to be sued for both breach of contract and tort liability.

Contract liability

A claim made against a consultant by a client could be based on the allegation that the consultant failed to perform the services described in the contract in a reasonable and prudent manner. This liability involves only those who are parties to the contract, and it applies whether there is a verbal contract, implied contract or written contract.

For the client to succeed in the claim against the consultant, all the following elements must be proved:

- There was a valid contract between the client and the consultant. This contract could be verbal or in writing.
- The consultant materially failed to perform his or her obligations under the contract.
- The client suffered damages as a result of the consultant's breach of obligation.

In actions brought under a breach of contract, it is irrelevant in most jurisdictions whether the consultant's breach was innocent, negligent or wilful. The client need only prove that a material breach of contract occurred and that damages resulted. There are, of course, numerous defences a consultant can raise, depending on the particular circumstances. The amount of damages assessed against the consultant would be an attempt to restore the client to the position held if the contract had not been breached.

A consultant can be sued for breach of contract, for example, if the precise duties and responsibilities or services required under the contract were not met exactly as detailed in the contract. This is a good reason to make certain that a contract is written, not verbal. In a verbal contract it is difficult to establish exactly what the terms of the agreement were.

Another example is a consultant who signed a fixed price contract for a service to be provided by a certain date. If the consultant miscalculated the fixed price and abandoned the project before it was completed, he or she could be sued. This is not uncommon among new consultants unfamiliar with the skill required in preparing a fixed price proposal.

Tort liability

Tort liability is a violation of civil law rather than a breach of contract. Liability in tort is incurred towards the public at large. Any third party who has suffered through the direct or indirect actions of the consultant can make a claim against the consultant, even if no contract existed with the consultant and the claimant had never met the consultant. For example, if a consultant submits a report with recommendations to a client and the client follows the recommendations, expends a large sum of money and subsequently loses the money, the client's creditors and investors and lenders could attempt to sue the consultant for losses suffered (damages) because of the negligent advice of the consultant. It would have to be shown that the consultant knew or reasonably should have known that others would be seeing the report with recommendations, and they would be relying on that report before investing or lending money.

For the claimant to succeed in a claim against the consultant, all the following elements must be proved:

- The consultant owed the claimant a duty of care.
- The duty or standard of care was breached.
- Measurable damages resulted from the breach.
- There was a direct connection between the breach of duty and the damages that occurred.

In a suit based on tort, evidence introduced into court must establish that the consultant departed from the local custom and standard of practice. If a consultant is found to be negligent, the court will attempt to compensate the claimant for the damages incurred.

Reasons for claims

Counterclaims
If a consultant sues a client to collect overdue fees, the client may counterclaim. The client may have a valid reason for not paying the fee, but very often the countersuit is intended to create delay and act as a leverage mechanism for settlement.

Conflict of interest
A consultant could be liable if it can be shown that the consultant had a vested interest in the outcome of the recommendations. For example, a client requests a computer consultant to review existing hardware and make recommendations for replacement. The consultant recommends replacement equipment. At some later point the client learns that the consultant received a payment from the distributor of the product line for recommending a very large order. The client could sue the consultant for the undisclosed profit; and, if it could be shown that the recommended hardware system was not the appropriate system in the circumstances, there could be additional liability on the consultant's part.

Conflicting interest of clients
A consultant could be working for two clients who are in competition with each other. If it can be shown that confidential information was disclosed or the benefits of assistance to one client was at the expense of the other, possible liability of the consultant could be present.

Delegation of part of contract to an employee or subconsultant
The primary consultant is responsible for the work of employees or agents under the primary consultant's control. If the client maintains that the consulting work was not done, or not done properly, by the

employee or subconsultant, legal action can be taken against the primary consultant.

Third-party damages

If a third party, such as a creditor, investor or lender, suffers damages as a consequence of the recommendations of the consultant to a second party, a third party can sue in tort.

Unclear expectations by client

It is possible that a client has unclear or unrealistic expectations of the work to be performed by the consultant and the benefit to the client. This lack of clarity can be a basis for dispute if the performance was not perceived to be related to expectations.

How to avoid professional liability and prevent losses

Although the possibility of being exposed to legal liability cannot be totally prevented, it can be substantially reduced by implementing effective administrative systems and procedures.

Many professionals concentrate on the technical aspects of their profession. Good management is equally important. Consideration must be given to proper staffing, training, credit and collection, and office procedures, such as keeping diaries, checklists and properly written records of every aspect and phase of the consulting business. Also, it is important to stay within the limits of your training, experience and expertise. Do not take on work that is beyond your capability.

Some good management techniques that can help to keep you out of trouble are discussed here.

Client control

Clients who try to avoid paying fees by claiming that errors have been made, or clients who resort to litigation can be costly for your business. Make sure that you have control over the areas for which you are responsible. In other words, do not assume responsibility for matters that your clients control.

You should implement a pre-screening process to select clients. Ways of pre-screening are covered in Chapter 6.

Cost quotations

Avoid giving quotations for activities arising from your services if possible. Depending upon the type of consulting practice you have, you could be locked into a situation where a fixed cost has been given and the

215

project suffers an overrun. Architects and engineers especially should avoid giving firm cost quotations.

Carefully drafted contracts

It is most important that a consultant operate with written contracts with clients. The contracts should be drafted carefully and based on competent legal advice. Contract ambiguities and misunderstandings are a major source of professional liability claims. Letters of understanding or contracts should be sent out to the client for acknowledgement and signature and returned by the client.

Free opinions

Be careful not to provide free opinions without knowing all the facts. You could be put in a position of being liable, even though you were not officially retained and had not received any fees. If it can be shown that someone relied on your advice, and subsequently suffered because of your advice, you could be held liable.

Law

Make sure you understand the law pertaining to your specific work. For example, if you are performing consulting assignments overseas, different laws may apply that could create problems for you.

Subconsultants

Subconsultants should be carefully selected. If appropriate, check to see that they carry adequate professional liability insurance. Make sure your insurance covers any work performed by a subconsultant.

Records, systems and procedures

Effective systems for files, records, invoicing and office procedures are essential for any business. See Chapter 17 for specific ideas on how to keep your records straight.

Continuing education

It is important that the consultant develops more expertise and training through various professional development and continuing education courses.

Quality control

The consultant should set up some system for monitoring the activities and performance of employees or subconsultants. If a system is in place, this will show that you have developed a high standard of care in the operation of your business.

Communication

Effective communication helps to eliminate many client problems. This topic is covered in Chapter 6.

Professional liability insurance

The procedures outlined in the previous section, if implemented, should substantially reduce the risk of professional liability. However, taking out professional liability insurance should be considered very carefully since the risk cannot be completely removed. Professional liability coverage should indemnify the consultant for losses and costs involved in the defence of claims. The Institute of Management Consultants has advised its members that professional indemnity insurance rates have risen steeply in recent years, and in the increasingly rigorous business climate it is essential that management consultants are adequately covered.

The liability insurance coverage is limited to claims arising from the performance of professional services including errors, omissions and negligent acts. If you provide a service outside the specified designation for your speciality, the insurance coverage could be voided.

There are many provisions in the policy that should be thoroughly explained, and if you are not completely satisfied, alternative coverage should be considered. The seven most important factors that have to be considered in selecting or analysing a professional liability insurance coverage are:

- Declarations
- Exclusions
- Insuring agreements
- Definitions
- Limits of liability
- Excess
- Policy conditions.

Your premiums can be reduced in a variety of ways, some of which are discussed here.

Excess

The greater the excess, the less expensive the policy premium should be. Check to see if the policy excess applies to each separate claim or just once a year.

Comparing prices

There is competition in the market-place for professional liability coverage. Make certain that the reduced premium presented to you does not reflect less attractive provisions in the policy that you may not understand. Professional advice should again be obtained from independent sources to satisfy yourself as to the nature of the coverage that you are getting. It is a prudent investment to ask a solicitor who specialises in insurance law to examine the proposed insurance terms and conditions.

Practising without insurance

Some consultants choose to conduct their business without any professional liability insurance. If the degree of exposure and risk is very low, this might be a viable alternative. If the consultant has very few personal assets and is effectively judgement proof, personal bankruptcy may be an alternative in the most extreme circumstances if a claim is made.

Incorporating a company and conducting the consulting practice through the company should add some protection in a lawsuit if the company lacks any assets. The danger of operating a consulting business that has a risk element but no professional liability insurance is the uncertainty if problems occur. A client or third party could sue the consultant personally as well as the company and, until the trial, you would not know what the outcome would be. In the meantime, you would have to incur the costs and pressure of the process. In other words, conducting a business through a company is not an automatic guarantee of personal protection. The other uncertainty is the nature and amount of damages that your advice caused your client or third parties. It may be very difficult to project at the time you are conducting a consulting assignment what the financial damages could be if your advice is in error.

If you do intend to practise without professional liability insurance, it is most important that you receive expert legal advice to maximise your protection in advance.

Appendices

Summary of the Code of Professional Conduct of the Institute of Management Consultants

The Institute's Code of Professional Conduct is structured on three basic principles dealing with:

1. High standards of service to the client;
2. Independence, objectivity and integrity;
3. Responsibility to the profession.

These principles are underpinned by a series of detailed rules and practical notes. The more important rules are summarised below. Copies of the full Code are available from the Institute office.

Principle 1: High standards of service to the client

A member shall carry out the duties he has undertaken for his client diligently, conscientiously and with due regard to the public interest.

A member will only accept an engagement for which he is suitably qualified.

The work to be carried out shall be clearly described and agreed in writing with the client. A member will not undertake work for a client unless he is satisfied that he has sufficient competent resources to carry it out effectively and efficiently; furthermore, he will undertake to hold all information concerning a client's affairs as strictly confidential.

A member will develop recommendations specifically for the solution of each client's problems. Such solutions shall be realistic and practicable and clearly understandable by the client. Furthermore, to ensure efficient performance of the assignment, the member will exercise good management through careful planning, frequent progress reviews and effective controls.

Principle 2: Independence, objectivity and integrity

A member will avoid any action or situation inconsistent with his

professional obligations or which in any way might be seen to impair his integrity.

For this purpose a member will maintain a fully independent position with the client at all times, making certain that advice and recommendations are based upon thorough and impartial consideration of all pertinent facts and circumstances and on opinion developed from reliable relevant experience.

A member will not serve a client in circumstances which might impair his independence, objectivity or integrity and will inform the client immediately should such circumstances arise during the course of an assignment; furthermore, he will reserve the right to withdraw if circumstances beyond his control develop to interfere with the successful conduct of the assignment.

A member will discuss and agree with the client any significant changes in the objectives, scope, approach, anticipated benefits or other aspects of the assignment which might arise during the course of carrying it out.

Principle 3: Responsibility to the profession

A member shall at all times conduct himself in a manner which will enhance the standing and public regard of the profession.

For this purpose he will ensure that his knowledge and skills are kept up to date and he will not knowingly or without permission use copyright material or proprietary data.

A member will negotiate agreements and charges for professional services only in a manner approved as ethical and professional by the Institute.

Proposal Evaluation Checklist

General factors

- Has the bidder responded with an appropriate technique or is he or she trying to fit the problem to a favourite technique?
- What priority will this project receive from the consultant? How important will it be to his or her firm?
- Does the proposal meet the terms of reference and the intended scope of the study?
- How useful or capable of implementation will the end product be?
- What degree of originality is present in the proposal?
- Are the submission of progress reports and presentation of interim briefings required? What progress reports and interim briefings are planned?
- What degree of direct consultant–client liaison is proposed? Does the consultant–client relationship include a training component for the client's personnel? What type of training is proposed?
- Is the proposed content of progress reports in accordance with the requirements of the client? Will progress reports contain a monthly statement of costs incurred, commitments and, if necessary, a revised estimate of total costs?
- When the project is completed, how does the consultant intend to hand over the project?
- What degree of follow-up and/or debriefing is proposed? To whom do the relevant data belong and what happens to them when the project is completed?

Past performance

- Is the usual business of the offerer closely related to the proposed work?
- Do the references to past experience include activities specifically related to the requirements of the proposed study?

- Has the proposer been honoured by professional societies because of his/her performance in a specific professional area?
- What reputation does the firm hold in the area of the proposed study?
- Has the firm worked for this client before, and if so with what success?
- Are the statements of past performance worded so you can identify what work was actually performed?
- Are there aspects of past performance that indicate particular weaknesses or strengths?

Scope of work

- Has the proposal demonstrated an understanding of the problems to be solved?
- Is this research area new to the company?
- Has the offerer made an accurate assessment of the problem based on an interpretation of the requirements set forth in the work statement?
- Has the offerer presented an approach that will achieve the stated objectives?
- Is the proposed approach supported with justification of why it should achieve the evaluation objectives?
- Do you think the suggested approach will work?
- Has the offerer introduced unanticipated events which may result in a project overrun or an expanded scope of work?
- Does the proposal distinguish between the simpler and the more difficult performance requirements?
- Does the proposal convincingly show a depth of understanding of the problem?
- Are the technical problems clearly delineated or are they merely 'parroted' from the proposal request?
- Have the limits of the problem been specified to show that the proposed study will be restricted to an appropriate scope?
- Is there a concise but adequate review of literature? Is the literature review merely an annotated bibliography or is it a scholarly critique?
- Are the specific objectives of the proposal clearly stated? Are these goals realistic in view of time, equipment, budget and professional experience of the principal investigator?
- Does the plan, in fact, permit an unequivocal test of the stated hypotheses of research questions?

- Does the proposal represent a unique, imaginative approach?
- Is the technical programme fully responsive to all written requirements and specifications?
- Are there any apparent discrepancies or omissions?
- Are 'products' clearly defined and presented?

Personnel

- Is it clear which tasks in the study specific personnel will be assigned to and for what amount of time?
- Are the personnel assigned to specific tasks qualified by training and experience to perform the tasks successfully?
- Is there a clear organisation chart depicting project management? Is there realistic apportionment of personnel level and time to specific tasks?
- What assurances are made concerning the availability of personnel proposed? Was a contingency plan requested if certain personnel become unavailable?
- Have enough time and personnel been included to provide adequate administrative management of the study?
- Is the author of the proposal one of the key personnel?
- Does the success of the project depend, to a large degree, upon personnel not directly associated with the prospective firm?
- Do CVs relate specific experience of personnel to the specific needs of this project?
- Does the proposal show the capabilities of the management to handle a project of the size contemplated?
- Is the position of the programme manager in the overall organisation and the limits of his or her authority and responsibility shown?
- Are the type, frequency and effectiveness of management controls and method for corrective action shown?
- Does the task organisation integrate the overall organisation in terms of effective lines of authority and communication, and in terms of effective integration of research, development, design, drafting, technical writing and, where appropriate, test functions?
- Is it clearly demonstrated that top-level management will maintain a high level of interest and assume responsibility for successful accomplishment of the programme?
- Is the proposal dependent upon recruitment of key personnel?

Planning and management

- Has the work schedule been specified clearly, and is it realistic in terms of time and money? Does it fit with available personnel?
- If time of performance is important and is a competitive evaluation factor, is the proposed schedule supported by the technical proposal?
- Is the planning realistic? Does it follow recognised and accepted procedure?
- Does the proposal show that the delivery schedule will be met and how it will be met?
- Is sufficient detail regarding master scheduling, programming, follow-up and other similar functions given to reinforce the foregoing assurance?
- Are the various technical phases of the project detailed and realistically scheduled?
- Are effective review, evaluation and control provided at specific checkpoints?
- Has the offerer allowed for all necessary clearances?

Facilities

- Are the facilities and equipment needed for successful completion of the study specified in the proposal?
- How does the offerer intend to access facilities not at the contractor's site?
- Does the use of facilities outside the contractor's firm require a subcontract? If so, is the proposed subcontractor specifically mentioned, along with an explanation of required qualifications?
- Is the planned use of facilities, such as printing, data processing etc realistic?
- If computer services are required, are there controls built into the processing so corrective action can be taken at intermittent points if necessary?
- Is any government-furnished equipment required?
- Are the proposed laboratory and test facilities adequate for the requirements of the technical scope of work?
- Are resources over-committed?

Cost

- Is the overall cost within range of your (the contracting agency's) budget?

- What is the relationship between the cost figures and equivalent items in the technical proposal?
- Are the personnel costs reasonable according to the tasks to be performed?
- Are the appropriate personnel assigned to perform the appropriate tasks?
- Has expenditure been set aside for subcontracting requirements, such as data processing?
- If a large-scale questionnaire must be mailed, has an adequate sum been set aside for postage?
- Have costs for development of instruments, purchase of materials, such as scoring sheets etc been included?
- Does the travel seem reasonable when compared to the tasks to be accomplished?
- If consultants or experts are included, is their daily rate reasonable and within the proper financial range? Is the proposed time reasonable?
- Is an appropriate type of contract requested?
- Is the schedule of payment acceptable?
- Have appropriate procedures been used to estimate costs?

Further Reading from Kogan Page

Setting up business

Choosing and Using Professional Advisers, editor Paul Chaplin, 1986
Funding Your Business, Kenneth Winckles, 1988
How to Choose Business Premises: A Guide for the Small Firm, Howard Green, Brian Chalkley and Paul Foley, 1986
How to Deal with Your Bank Manager, Geoffrey Sales, 1988

Running the business

The Guardian Guide to Running a Small Business, editor Clive Woodcock, 7th edition, 1988
Working for Yourself: The Daily Telegraph Guide to Self-Employment, Godfrey Golzen, 10th edition, 1988

Finance, tax and legal

Finance and Accounts for Managers, Desmond Goch, 1986
Financial Management for the Small Business, 2nd edition, Colin Barrow, 1988
Law for the Small Business: The Daily Telegraph Guide, 6th edition, Patricia Clayton, 1988
Solving Business Cash Problems, CT Edge, 1988
The Stoy Hayward Business Tax Guide, Mavis Seymour and Stephen Say (annual)

Promotion and marketing

The Accountant's Guide to Practice Promotion, Patrick Forsyth, 1988
Commonsense Direct Marketing, Drayton Bird, 1989
How to Promote Your Own Business, Jim Dudley, 1987
Marketing for Accountants and Managers, R J Williamson, 3rd edition, 1988

Successful Marketing for the Small Business: The Daily Telegraph Guide,
2nd edition, Dave Patten, 1988

Personal skills

The Business Guide to Effective Speaking, Jacqueline Dunckel and Elizabeth
Parnham, 1985
The Business Guide to Effective Writing, JA Fletcher and DF Gowing,
1987
Improving Your Presentation Skills, Michael Stevens, 1987
Report Writing in Business, Trevor J Bentley, 1987

Useful Addresses

Management consultancy, organisations and registers

British Consultants Bureau
Westminster Palace Gardens
1-7 Artillery Road
London SW1P 7RJ
Tel: 01-222 3651

Directory of Management
Consultants in the UK
TFPL Publishing
76 Park Road
London NW1 4SH
Tel: 01-258 3740

IM Register of Marketing
Consultants
Institute of Marketing
Moor Hall
Cookham
Berkshire SL6 9QH
Tel: 06285 24922

Institute of Management
Consultants
5th Floor
32-33 Hatton Garden
London EC1N 8DL
Tel: 01-242 2140

Management Consultants
Association
11 West Halkin Street
London SW1X 8JL
Tel: 01-235 3897

Management Consultancy
Information Service
38 Blenheim Avenue
Gants Hill
Ilford
Essex IG2 6SQ
Tel: 01-554 4695

Management Organisations

British Institute of Management
Management House
Cottingham Road
Corby
Northants NN17 1TT
Tel: 0536 204222

Institute of Directors
116 Pall Mall
London SW1Y 5ED
Tel: 01-839 1233

Institute of Marketing
Moor Hall
Cookham
Maidenhead
Berkshire SL6 9QH
Tel: 06285 24922

Institute of Personnel Management
IPM House
35 Camp Road
Wimbledon
London SW19 4UW
Tel: 01-946 9100

Institute of Training and
Development
5 Baring Road
Beaconsfield
Buckinghamshire HP9 2NX
Tel: 04946 3994

Government and International Agencies and Organisations

Advisory Conciliation and
Arbitration Service
27 Wilton Street
London SW1X 7AZ
Tel: 01-210 3600

The British Council
10 Spring Gardens
London SW1A 2BN
Tel: 01-930 8466

International Labour Office
96-98 Marsham Street
London SW1P 4LY
Tel: 01-828 6401

Organisation for Economic
Cooperation and Development
2 Rue Andre-Pascal
75775 Paris 16
France
Tel: 5248200

United Nations Information Centre
Ship House
20 Buckingham Gate
London SW1E 6LB
Tel: 01-630 1981

World Bank
181 H Street NW
Washington DC 20433
USA

London Office:
New Zealand House
Haymarket
London SW1Y 4TE
Tel: 01-930 3886

Index